So You Want to Be an Inclusive Leader?

Five Simple Strategies You Can Use to Inclusify Your Workplace

By Dr. Jonathan King

ISBN: 9798357865724

DEDICATION

This book is dedicated to the loving memory of my parents, Slater and Marion King, who were the first to model the principles of inclusive leadership in my life. I also want to express my gratitude to my wife Esther and our children Kamal and Shoghi for inspiring me to finish this writing project from beginning to end. I love you to the moon and back!

CONTENTS

INTRODUCTION

My boyhood dream to become an All-Star NFL running back unfortunately did not pan out as I had envisioned. Despite the fact that I had become a High School All-American in Football and was the Captain of my football team, I stood at only 5 feet eight inches and weighed a measly 160 lbs. Unfortunately, I lacked the required speed and size to become a superstar among my peers and follow in the footsteps of the great running backs I had grown up admiring like Jim Brown and Gayle Sayers. It became very clear to me after I graduated from High School that my chances of going to the Pros was extremely unlikely, but my chances of making it as a Businessmen was highly probable due to the fact that a growing number of Fortune 500 companies were beginning to hire people of color in the mid 1970's. After graduating from Thompson's Academy, a boarding school located on Thompson's Island in South Boston, Massachusetts, I found myself pursuing a Business Management degree at Morehouse College, a prestigious all-male black College (Historically Black College or University) in Atlanta Georgia whose most famous graduate was none other than Dr. Martin Luther King. Initially, my goal was to graduate and eventually take over my parent's real estate business in my hometown, Albany, Georgia, however, extenuating circumstances dictated otherwise; my father's unexpected death – and an unexpected economic recession – brought our family business to a quick and unfortunate end.

With few resources at my disposal, I was forced to travel a different path towards economic security. Given that minorities – in particular African Americans – had begun to land entry-level positions at Fortune 500 companies like Coca-Cola and Delta Airlines during the early 1980's, I decided to pursue a management position in corporate America. To say that was a difficult mountain to climb is an understatement. Luckily, my Aunt Totsie (formerly known as Dr. Jennye Harland), who worked at Clark Atlanta University (formerly Clark College) as the Director of Business Internships, was able to secure five separate internship opportunities over a five year period. In each of these placements except one, I was the only Black person in the room – a trend that continued for much of my career.

The positive side of being the first person of color hired into an all-White organization was that it afforded me the opportunity to experience the challenges inherent in a non-inclusive workplace. My internship experiences were the starting point from which I rose to become a leader in the diversity and inclusion (D&I) space, not only in the United States, but also as far away as Asia, where I became the very first foreigner to work for Warner International Japan and Sony Entertainment Japan.

Although I have witnessed the rapid growth of workplace diversity over my 30 plus years of working in a number of public and private agencies throughout the United States, it goes without saying that most organizations are still plagued by realities of structural racism and unconscious bias. Despite the fact that a growing number of Fortune 500 executives understand how swiftly workplaces are becoming more diverse– collectively – they have failed to make their work environments more inclusive and welcoming in response.

Despite the fact that U.S. companies now spend over $8 billion a year on DEI programs, HR executives across from across the United States claim that their workplaces – as reported by their employees of color – lack a true sense of belonging. Research indicates that when employees lack a sense of belonging in the organization, and do not feel valued for what they bring to the table, their companies suffer in the areas of team development, innovation, and overall company profitability.

A 2020 McKinsey & Company report[1] found that while 52% of employees felt positive about their company's diversity efforts, only 29% felt they were performing well with efforts at inclusion. The research shows that even the largest corporations – those with the biggest budgets – struggle with achieving inclusion for their employees of color. It also indicates that companies remain better at hiring people of color than do at promoting them, and despite pouring billions each year into the big, shiny D&I bucket, positive advancement and promotion outcomes for minorities remain stuck in the past.

Racial Representation in Fortune 500 Companies

Another study from McKinsey and LeanIn.org tells a similarly disappointing story. A look at racial representation in entry-level and management positions at top-tier Fortune 500 companies shows that White people hold 65 percent of entry-level roles in corporate America, while people of color represent only 32 percent. The inequity steadily increases at higher levels of management. Whites account for 81 percent of VP positions compared with only 19 percent for people of color. In the C-suite, the numbers are even more stark. White men hold 68 percent of all positions, with White women accounting for 18 percent, and women of color only 4%. Only three Black CEOs show up in the Fortune 500 realm.

The pace of organizational change remains frustratingly slow, but larger societal changes are pushing D&I issues to the forefront. With the rise of various ethnic and cultural groups in mainstream society over the past 30 years – namely Black, LatinX, women, LGBTQ, and immigrants – companies that have chosen to remain non-inclusive have faced the combined forces of social condemnation and legal judgements – which has been costly and embarrassing for all stakeholders involved.

The Death of George Floyd and the Rise of Inclusivity

Before the death of George Floyd, there existed an expressed belief that the United States had entered a post-racial era – that the threat of racial polarization had ended. When the United States elected its first Black president in 2008, many held the false impression that racial injustices had somehow disappeared. A look at hate-crime statistics tells a different story; despite the political, economic, and social advances made by Blacks and other minorities, hate crimes against visible minorities – against Jews and Blacks especially – increased exponentially. A prime example of this is when Dylan Roof brutally murdered nine African American church members at the Emanuel African Methodist Church in Charleston, South Carolina, and subsequently, a deadly Pennsylvania synagogue attack left 11 dead. Many other houses of worship were threatened and vandalized in the backlash of racial hate sparked by the election of a Black President – an unsettling trend that further escalated with Donald Trump's 2017 election.

The Rise of the BLM and the # MeToo Movement

Just as the brutal 1953 killing of Emmett Till in Money, Mississippi, led to the launch of a civil rights movement in Montgomery, Alabama, Floyd's death lit a raging inferno of inter-racial global protest. Powered by social media platforms that had not existed during the birth of the civil rights era, the

Black Lives Matter Movement quickly spread its wings. It became the new face of opposition to racial discrimination in all forms. While the murders of Till and Floyd were similar, the aftermaths of their deaths were starkly different. The crowds attending Black Lives Matter protest marches in the wake of Floyd's death were largely multi-racial, and they marched across the globe simultaneously.

This unprecedented use of social media made it possible for people to coordinate events on a global scale in ways that were unthinkable just one generation ago. It did much the same with raising awareness and bringing race to the forefront of social conversation. Nevertheless, despite the growing openness amongst Whites to discussing the realities of racism in and out of the workplace, most companies continued to merely pay lip service to diversity and inclusion. Behind the curtain of diversity ad campaigns, corporate leaders do not have a clear vision about how to make their companies more inclusive. The non-inclusive style of management that existed before Floyd's death continues to operate – albeit under a veil of silence.

The purpose of writing this book is to share my humble insights on how leaders within all types of organizations (public/ private/ big/small), can re-shift their priorities and invest in making their workplaces more inclusive by removing any remaining vestiges of systemic racism and unconscious bias.

The Five Step Plan – The ADAPT Inclusion Model

When the 'how' is absent, it is almost impossible to find ways to remove negative biases and achieve unity and understanding. What follows in these pages is the 'how' – a simple, five-step program called ADAPT – aimed at helping leaders, managers, and employees create more joyful, inclusive, and inter-culturally collaborative work environments. The ADAPT model guides us through confronting and removing our internal biases – whatever our early programming. Following the steps of this program will help us build awareness and become more inclusive leaders, while giving us the requisite skills to become powerful workplace agents of change. Let's get started!

CHAPTER 1
WHAT IS INCLUSIVITY AND WHY DOES IT MATTER?

Back when I was growing up, the term inclusivity had not yet been coined. It was not until the early 1980's that new employment legislation mandated that companies could no longer discriminate against applicants based on the color of their skin. These new laws brought a sudden and tumultuous end to segregation. Although Blacks and Whites had previously worked separately for the same institutions – in hospitals where there were White and Black wards for instance – for the most part, minorities had not been allowed to work directly with Whites in professional occupations like teaching, business, or the tech industry.

Like a sudden tidal wave, civil rights act of 1964 swept away segregated workplaces and allowed people of color – who had been previously restricted to primarily low-paying, blue-collar jobs – to begin climbing the corporate ladder. The integration of America became the zeitgeist of that era, giving minorities the feeling that anything was possible. There was the belief that any person who worked hard enough – no matter what their color or race – could advance in their career without limitation.

Integration was portrayed as a social elixir capable of healing the wounds and injustices that had resulted from workplace discrimination.

At that point, the idea of creating a welcoming work environment, and engendering a sense of belonging among people of color was not on anyone's radar. If it was discussed at all, it was only in the ivory towers of Higher Education. That began to change, however, as minorities increasingly began to pursue the high-paying, specialized careers that had traditionally been reserved for their White counterparts. Within a short time, companies found themselves facing the challenge of ensuring that employees of all cultural and ethnic backgrounds were treated equitably. However, their largely White male management teams were not adequately trained to manage and interact with employees of diverse cultural backgrounds, so racial and sexual harassment began to increase. A significant uptick in employment discrimination lawsuits followed the rise of minorities in the workplace – making it clear that increased workplace diversity did not automatically lead to minorities receiving equal treatment or advancement opportunities.

Initially, companies expected the transition to be brief – that culturally divergent employees would soon become acclimated to their organization's culture. Workplace statistics showed otherwise though, and the number of lawsuits involving racial discrimination and bias escalated exponentially over a 15-year period. Even today, despite U.S. companies pouring billions of dollars into diversity programs aimed at recruiting and training people of color, positive outcomes around overall retention and advancement remain low.

So Much Money, So Little Progress

How can so much money be spent on promoting diversity in the workplace result in such little progress with increasing retention and advancement opportunities for employees of color? My experience as a DEI practitioner points to three key reasons:

1. In both large and small organizations, HR departments are usually at the heart of determining what money is spent on the recruitment and onboarding of new employees of color. Unfortunately, they invest little on comprehensive training for managers about how to successfully manage diverse work teams.

2. Leaders are rarely asked for input on how DEI spending could best meet the needs of their workplaces. At best, they are informed at the end of the DEI activity planning process how the money will be spent. The primary decision-makers allocating funds are C-Suite and HR leaders – two groups who do not typically have a finger on the pulse of interdepartmental workings. Though managers are generally

put through an annual unconscious-bias workshop, there is typically no further training on how to overcome unconscious biases or deal with the complexities of diversity in the workplace.

3. DEI Goals are not created organically from the very workplaces and departments where employees of color work. Without such goals, HR and C-Suite leaders have little foresight on their workplace needs around diversity and equity. They also lack any way to determine if real progress has been made with ensuring that employees are being treated equally.

What does this have to do with Inclusivity? It goes to show that no matter how much is spent on promoting diversity in the workplace, if inclusivity is lacking, employees of color will not feel a sense of well-being, and in turn, they will not be as productive as their White counterparts. Furthermore, when there is a lack of trust and employees do not feel psychologically safe, they tend to seek opportunities elsewhere.

Lastly – but perhaps most importantly – when companies do not cultivate inclusive leadership on their management teams, they achieve little in the way of promoting overall inclusivity. Employees of color do not waste time waiting for a sense of belonging to materialize, opting instead to search for hope and solace at other companies. In addition, companies who fail to develop inclusive leaders achieve low retention rates with employees of color. They also tend to face increased levels of complaints involving sexual and racial harassment.

The Many Benefits of Inclusivity

So what do we need to know about companies that are purposely inclusive versus companies that lack inclusivity? In a recent McKinsey and Company report[2], data taken from thousands of companies across 15 countries showed that companies performing in the top quarter for gender and cultural diversity on their executive teams were 25 percent more likely to have above average profitability than companies in the bottom quarter – a number which grew from 21 percent in 2017 and 15 percent in 2014. Another study by Boston Consulting Group[3] revealed that increasing the diversity of leadership teams led to corresponding increases in innovation and financial performance. They also found that companies with more diverse management report 19 per cent higher revenue due to innovation.

Other key factors uncovered by researchers about inclusive work environments were that individual employees were more productive on the job than employees in non-inclusive work environments, and they tended to thrive and get promoted more quickly within the organization. The same can be said for diverse work teams. Not only were they found to be more productive and innovative, but they also stood out as being more profitable when compared to non-diverse work teams. Research from the study 'Great Place to Work', showed that companies with consistently inclusive workplaces thrived before, during, and after the Great Recession of 2008-2010, earning a 4x annualized return.[4]

While workplace diversity is sometimes viewed from the narrow perspective of culture, race, and ethnicity, the multi-dimensional complexity of diversity can be expanded to include the full spectrum of physical, mental, and philosophical differences we see in humans across the globe. Because we now have the tools to work virtually and share skills and technologies without meeting face-to-face, it is more imperative than ever that companies focus on being more inclusive.

A recent Harvard Business Review study[5] described the most successful teams as having cognitive diversity – with team members who engage in different ways of thinking and decision-making and who are given the freedom to be creative with solutions. Companies that fail to adopt this level of diversity rob themselves of significant benefits and place themselves at a disadvantage with their competitors. If companies want to be more productive, innovative, and profitable, they need to prioritize becoming more inclusive.

When Not Becoming Inclusive Becomes an Added Cost

One major reason that non-inclusive companies continue to lag behind more diverse companies with employee job satisfaction, productivity, innovation, and overall profitability is that they consider workplace inclusion as a cost rather than an investment. While HR can help, the key driver of emotional and psychological security among diverse employees is the workplace leader. Before that can happen, however, companies need to consider one of the biggest barriers to achieving inclusivity – eliminating unconscious bias.

You may wonder – how serious is 'unconscious bias'? On a scale of 1 to 10, I would rank it between 8 and 10, but depending on who you ask, you'll hear differing responses. Some may say that unconscious bias is not real; others feel it has minimal impact on building inclusive work environments, and some consider it relevant but not overly serious. What I have witnessed – and still continue to experience – is racial and ethnic prejudice not only in the workplace, but in my day-to-day interactions while running errands, while visiting the bank and being asked to show identification, even while having people behind me in line be served ahead of me.

Companies are microcosms of society, and the racial, cultural, and gender biases that have existed in workplaces for hundreds of years still exist today. Although we have come a long way in changing our attitudes, our deep-seated biases remain alive and well, regardless of what HR might say about having zero tolerance discrimination policies. That being said, our biases have become more nuanced, and we now hold them against others who are transgender, LGBTQ, neurodiverse, who have learning disabilities, or are physically handicapped. Ageism also enters into the mix. Moreover, as employment discrimination continues to rear its ugly head, the number of lawsuits filed by victims who claim their rights have been violated continues to grow. In addition to the unfair treatment these victims have faced, they are, in many cases, forced to leave their companies under the pretext that they were not a good fit, or that they found better employment elsewhere.

In most cases, it has been HR departments responsible for providing managers with specialized training on why they should not discriminate. However, they have aimed no such programs towards rooting out unconscious bias, which remains one of the most challenging barriers to building an inclusive work environment where employees feel safe and psychologically secure. DEI experts today believe that managers – not HR – must take hold of this mantle of leadership. Instead of playing a defensive role, they must proactively change their behaviors to fulfill the requirements of bringing equity to their workplaces.

Lawsuits Can be Deadly Costly

My experience of working in multiple workplaces throughout the world has shown me that most people strive to be good employees and leaders. However, it is also clear that most companies do not adequately prepare their employees – especially those of the 'baby boom' generation – to welcome and support others who do not share their cultural and ethnic backgrounds. One experience stands out in my mind: I was hired right out of college to work in the baggage claim area for a major Atlanta airline. Our team – mostly White and Black men – loaded and unloaded planes every other hour and although the workspace was beginning to shift from being all White to nearly half Black, there was little interaction between the two groups of workers. We resembled two work camps, with Whites passing their time together playing board games and cards, while Blacks kept to themselves doing pretty much the same. Blacks and Whites only worked side-by-side when it was necessary for four people to climb into the belly of a plane to quickly unload and reload baggage within a 30-minute period. It was backbreaking work performed mostly in silence. It was uncommon to see Blacks and Whites sitting together unless they were watching television together in the main break room. When there was a disagreement about what program to watch, the White employees were given a separate break room, which Blacks were not allowed to enter.

As workplaces become more ethnically diverse, it is difficult for some to wrap their heads around the fact that differences of opinion, race, gender, sexual orientation, and ethnicity should be recognized and embraced. A refusal to do so often results in the type of toxic environments which breed sexual, racial, and ethnic harassment.

When Inclusivity is Lacking

When leaders are not intentionally inclusive on a day-to-day basis, it creates disunity and distrust in the workplace, especially between workers from diverse cultural backgrounds. It becomes highly problematic when a manager – one who lacks a diverse cultural background – does not intentionally understand the impact of his or her implicit bias on others of a different cultural background. It sets a precedent for unacceptable behaviors, which if not challenged or rectified, can ultimately lead to the kind of unforeseen grievances that erode morale and goodwill.

In my 20+ years as a manager in Higher Education, I have been continually exposed to non-inclusive workplaces. During that time, one Hispanic-serving College in San Diego stands out in particular for its unwillingness to acknowledge the unfair treatment of Black employees by LatinX managers at several levels of the organization. Over the years, several shocking incidents occurred, including one where people in the department placed banana peels near the Black employees' lockers.

At one point, someone even hung a noose in the area – a matter that was not fully investigated by management or HR. When Black employees approached the only Black dean on campus to seek her advice and assistance, she drafted a letter on their behalf to the President and Vice Presidents to highlight the seriousness of their charge. Without meeting with her to review the claims, she was put on immediate administrative leave, and her computer was confiscated and never returned.

Over the next three years, more incidents like this took place, eventually leading to over 30 lawsuits being filed against the college. By that time, it was a mess too large to clean up and the College eventually settled the lawsuits out of court at a tremendous expense of $20+ million. DEI consultants were also contracted for conflict mediation, at the additional expense of millions of dollars as well. An ensuing report labelling the environment as an anti-Black institution resulted not only in bad publicity for the college, but it further eroded the trust of Black students in the community. These negative outcomes could have been avoided had the leaders taken the higher road, acknowledged the need to confront systemic racism, and worked to train, educate, and eradicate the biases standing in the way of equity in the workplace and classroom.

Other companies recently hit with racial harassment lawsuits for their unwillingness to be inclusive are Tesla, which had to pay an employee $125 million dollars for allowing him to be racially victimized by managers for over a year, Walmart, which was forced to pay $4 million over a non-inclusive interaction that a store employee had with a customer of color, and Google, which had a multi-million-dollar class action lawsuit filed against them for not fairly promoting its Black employees. The list goes on. All in all, it is estimated that non-inclusive U.S. companies are forced to pay over one billion dollars each year in racial and gender harassment lawsuits – costs that could be avoided with the right focus on specialized training and intentional education.

CHAPTER TWO
THE SIX+ TRAITS OF
AN INCLUSIVE LEADER

While interning with the U.S. Department of Labor in Atlanta during my college days, I worked in a division responsible for overseeing funding for city and county agencies in Georgia and Florida. Representatives from our department traveled each week to a different part of Florida to ensure funds were neither misused nor misappropriated – work which my immediate supervisor (Bobby Hunter), who was also Black, did not want me directly involved in. From the day he took over as my boss, he acted like I was a nuisance – never taking me out to lunch or making any effort to get to know me. It seemed as though he was almost embarrassed at the prospect of having me accompany him at work. It looked like I would spend my entire summer doing little more than sitting at a desk. I was grateful to earn the seasonal income, and to add the job experience to my resume, but otherwise, it seemed that the internship would be a waste of my time.

After two weeks of doing very little, however, things took an interesting turn when I was approached by the executive leader of the group (David Epson) – a man in his 60's who happened to be White. Despite the fact that he and I had little in common, he took the time to get to know me – asking about my experience so far with the internship and about what my intentions were after college. The difference in our ages and cultural backgrounds didn't prevent him from taking an interest in me. Declaring that he wanted me to see what his team was doing in the field, he made the executive decision to invite me on the weekly out-of-state trips to various parts of Florida. I can still remember the look on my Black boss's face when my new White mentor said I should join all the summer trips to gain experience in case the department hired me on after graduation.

That summer I ended up learning a lot about how the U.S. Department of Labor operates. More importantly, however, I came away with an understanding of how to model inclusion in a way that makes everyone feel welcomed and appreciated. That White leader had no obligation to spend time with me, but he went out of his way to create the opportunity for me to develop into a future leader. He remains one of my biggest heroes to this day – and I thrived as a result of his inclusive leadership.

What Is an Inclusive Leader by Definition?

Although there are many definitions, I think the one that best summarizes the characteristics of an inclusive leader, no matter what organizational setting they work in, is this:

An inclusive leader is a person responsible for overseeing diversity, equity, inclusion, and belonging (sometimes shortened to DEIB) in the work environment, and who models positive behaviors to support diverse teams and foster an environment where people feel uniquely valued and included.

Becoming an inclusive leader goes far beyond having the desire to create an inclusive work environment because it is socially popular or 'the right thing to do.' As workplaces become increasingly diverse, inclusive leaders must be deeply involved with their teams – doing the necessary work to learn about the needs of their employees – especially those who are different culturally, ethnically, or otherwise.

Becoming an Inclusive Leader – Important Considerations

The first step on the path to becoming an authentic inclusive leader involves self-reflection about your attitudes and beliefs around diversity, equity, and inclusion with the aim of understanding how to better cultivate inclusion amongst your employees.

Some important things to consider as you begin this journey include:

- **It's a marathon, not a sprint.** Though some managers expect to visit a bookstore, read a few books, and turn into an inclusive leader overnight, they soon discover that learning about cultural differences cannot be accomplished by reading a few books.

- **It won't be quick.** This is a continuous process of lifelong learning. Accepting the fact that our own culture is not the center of the universe involves admitting that other cultures are unique and special in their own way. This realization can't occur within the confines of a book or series of webinars.

- **You're going to learn a lot** – about other cultures, ethnic groups, and peoples. Leveraging recent technological advantages allows us to instantly meet people from all over the globe – affording us endless opportunities to learn about other cultures.

- **It won't be easy.** You will have to face your own implicit bias – which some people find difficult to do. Once you realize that you were socially programmed to be prejudiced for or against others though, you will be better able to let go of the blame typically attached to admitting your unconscious biases exist.

- **It will require deep commitment on your part to supporting equity for every one of your employees.** Once you begin to learn about the advantages and disadvantages facing each cultural group in the workplace, you will be better positioned as a leader to help every member of your team thrive under all circumstances.

Traits of an Inclusive Leader as Defined by Deloitte

While there has been much written about inclusive leadership, the article, "The Six Traits of an Inclusive Leader," by Deloitte Consulting Group really stands out.[6] As an inclusive leadership practitioner, I see their six signature traits of an inclusive leader (The six C's) as an ideal launching pad from which managers can begin assessing their own strengths and weaknesses:

1. **Courage**: Showing vulnerability and taking some personal risk
2. **Cognizance**: Becoming aware of your own biases
3. **Curiosity**: Being curious about others' differences
4. **Cultural Competency**: Becoming culturally aware and accepting of other cultures
5. **Collaboration**: Working directly with others who don't share the same culture
6. **Commitment**: Being dedicated to creating and cultivating organizational inclusion

Figure 1. The six signature traits of an inclusive leader

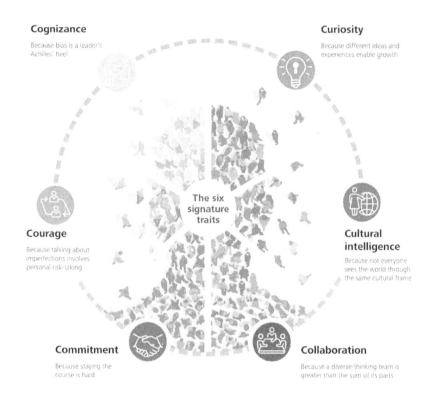

Cognizance
Because bias is a leader's
Achilles' heel

Curiosity
Because different ideas and
experiences enable growth

The six
signature
traits

Courage
Because talking about
imperfections involves
personal risk-taking

Cultural
intelligence
Because not everyone
sees the world through
the same cultural frame

Commitment
Because staying the
course is hard

Collaboration
Because a diverse-thinking team is
greater than the sum of its parts

Graphic: Deloitte University Press | DUPress.com

Cognizance and Courage

Of Deloitte's six signature traits, the one most important to begin with is Cognizance, as managers must understand their own biases before they can embark on the path of becoming a successful inclusive leader. This will be easier for some than others – some leaders will easily identify and admit to their own biases, while others may struggle with admitting what they consider to be weaknesses.

To have any hope of success, they must also concentrate on developing courage to see them through the discomfort of appearing vulnerable in the eyes of their direct reports and teammates. That courage will also help them with admitting that diverse perspectives exist in the workplace and that they do not know everything there is to know about other cultures. From a foundation of strength in cognizance and courage, managers can then begin developing the other four C's of Deloitte's list.

Curiosity, Cultural Intelligence, Collaboration, and Commitment

To stay on top of all of the cultural differences in today's workplace experience, inclusive leaders must stay curious about other cultures, view each worker as an individual, and not assume that because they are Black, White, or other, that their background can be comprehensively understood. Managers should expand their reading lists to help with learning about each new cultural group they encounter.

While reading and watching videos about other cultures is commendable, the aim is to move to being skilled in interacting with others through close-up association and collaboration. As leaders become more culturally inquisitive, they will naturally begin to interact with other cultural groups more easily. That will ultimately lead to locking arms and working with culturally diverse employees instead of limiting interactions to nothing more than quick smiles and polite greetings.

Lastly, inclusive managers must view this process as a never-ending marathon. They must show commitment to supporting and embracing diversity and equity, and work tirelessly to create inclusive environments wherever they work.

Other Traits of an Inclusive Leader

Beyond Deloitte's six signature traits, I believe that making environments more inclusive requires two additional traits:

7. **Treat all people in the workplace equitably and equally**: Managers must ensure that opportunities given to one group of employees are offered to all. This involves ensuring that his or her own group does not receive preferential treatment due to cultural affinities and similarities.

8. **Practice and promote equity**: Groups that have typically been disenfranchised or marginalized must be provided with training opportunities aimed at helping them access jobs that were once denied to them because of racial, ethnic, or social differences. Managers should also take steps to close any existing equity gaps in their workplace.

Barriers to Becoming an Inclusive Leader

Building inclusive work environments may be trending currently in the United States but that does not necessarily mean all your team members will be open to participating in that exercise. Some might openly resist having the program pushed on them in what they consider a 'top-down' decision. They may voice outright opposition to participating or simply refuse to consider that they hold any implicit biases. You may need to hold one-on-one meetings with the people or factions opposed to the idea. Whatever it takes, it is your job as leader to sell them on the benefits of inclusivity.

Another potential obstacle may come from an unexpected place – it is possible that you may encounter opposition from the visible minorities on your team. Some of them may have grown weary due to previously broken promises to expand equity in the workplace. You may end up sandwiched between these two different groups who see the prospect of change from two very different perspectives. The dominant group may see inclusivity as a barrier to their privilege, while the minorities may see only empty promises.

Mediating Conflict with External Consultants

It may prove difficult to act as a mediator from your position as the leader. To work towards unraveling the feathers of opposition, it may be wise to step back from the conflict and recruit a paid DEI facilitator to communicate the importance of change, to explain how the process will work, and to set out clear benchmarks of how your organization's inclusivity goals will be met over the following one to three years. If the facilitator encounters opposition, you will need to step up and have sideline conversations about the importance of this mission, and to explain that it has the backing of your executive leadership team.

Nevertheless, there may be continued attempts at disruption, or even passive-aggressive attempts to undermine the process by threatening people of color. Be on the lookout as well for microaggressions aimed at causing people to feel humiliated and disenfranchised. If the team members creating this disunity do not fall into line, you will have to act – following courageous conversations with progressive disciplinary action to ensure the process does not become derailed.

Relying on Data to Prove the Importance of Inclusivity

You may be confronted with disruptions from team members during DEI meetings. They may insist that efforts at DEI are a waste of time, or they may claim the shift will not benefit the entire group. To respond effectively, you must be prepared. Having data at your fingertips is the only way to politely refute ignorant statements and opinions from vociferous members of the group who refuse to participate. While it is important that employees feel they have a voice and can express their doubts, in the end, this process has your company's backing – and the show must go on.

Getting Buy-In is Crucial

If you leave resistant employees to their own devices, you will likely fail to create an inclusive work environment. Every team member must contribute to the efforts to become a more inclusive department – a fact you must clearly communicate. To demonstrate how crucial it is that everyone move towards transformative change, their efforts at modeling inclusive behavior should be tied to future performance evaluations. This is best conveyed not as a threat, but rather as an agreement that everyone, including those in leadership, is expected to change, adopt inclusive behaviors, and help make the workplace a haven of emotional and psychological security for all.

Use Monthly Events to Bring People Together

Work environments can be toxic on many levels, beyond just the inequities of race, culture, and gender. A great way to chip away at your workplace's subtle divides and shift your team members out of their comfort zones is to start holding special monthly events. Ideally, you can arrange for people to meet over food and fun without requiring them to leave the workspace and pay for entertainment. People love to eat, and a delicious free lunch is hard to turn down. You could even organize a monthly potluck where everyone contributes either a dish or a drink, or a performance of poetry, music, or song.

Events like these encourage people to leave their desks and interact in a shared space with team members from different cultural backgrounds, creating a sense of unity among group members who do not know each other intimately. Scooping up a taco or a meatball made by someone else in the room helps people make connections they would not normally experience. Do not be afraid to focus your events on a specific theme, or to let people come up with their own ideas – themes could involve anything from Marvel comics to Women's Recognition month. The idea is to bring people together to forge new connections.

The connections made in these meetings, though brief, will introduce people to others with whom they can start building relationships, leading to future lunches together, shared project work, or even volunteer work together in the larger community and within outside networks both regionally and beyond. The breeding ground of belonging and inclusion begins with a spark of connection, and from there, the foundation of DEI principles can better take root.

CHAPTER 3
THE ADAPT MODEL – A FIVE-STEP STRATEGY TO BECOMING AN INCLUSIVE LEADER

The ADAPT model lays out a road map for transformative behavioral workplace change by providing a framework for managers and leaders to become more inclusive within their organization. These efforts do not have to be done in coordination with a Human Resources department, nor do they absolutely have to be undertaken in concert with other people in the department, but engaging all of a department's employees simultaneously generally does lead to more beneficial outcomes for the workplace as a whole. What is key above all is that the manager embarking on this step is fully engaged and committed to the process, as he or she will be the pioneer and champion of the effort to make the company more inclusive. With a departmental leader as point person, the program will gain traction and become a vehicle that all employees can utilize.

Though the ADAPT model is a five-step strategy, participants should understand from the outset that becoming an inclusive leader is an evolutionary process. Overcoming our biases is an ongoing process involving continuous, lifelong learning.

ADAPT Model for Becoming an Inclusive Leader

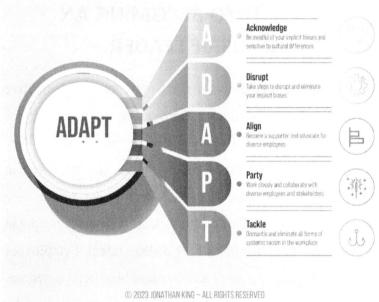

ADAPT

Acknowledge
- Be mindful of your implicit biases and sensitive to cultural differences

Disrupt
- Take steps to disrupt and eliminate your implicit biases

Align
- Become a supporter and advocate for diverse employees

Party
- Work closely and collaborate with diverse employees and stakeholders

Tackle
- Dismantle and eliminate all forms of systemic racism in the workplace

Step #1 – A for Acknowledge

The first – and arguably most powerful – step in the ADAPT process is acknowledging that we all have deep-seated biases that were imparted to us during childhood. Research has shown that by the time a child is 5 years old, their most hard-wired beliefs have been cemented in their subconscious. These ideas and prejudices became the foundation of our biases, which, like bacteria, remain ever-present in the deep recesses of our subconscious. Although we may be unaware of the innumerable biases floating around in our brains, the harmful ideas do indeed exist. Moreover, just as an alcoholic will fail to adequately address their alcohol abuse until they first acknowledge their problem, so too must we face up to our implicit biases if we have any hope of eradicating them.

How do we begin to take this step in a way that is authentically aligned with becoming more inclusive and transforming our work environment? We first must acknowledge that our biases exist within our subconscious, and then move to understand that our biases do not make us bad people, but that they can be harmful when used against people in the work environment. To that end, we must further acknowledge that we lack awareness around the ways and customs of all different groups of people. To make our workplace more inclusive and welcoming we will need to significantly broaden our learning.

Once these three acknowledgments are made, we will be ready to move forward with becoming a champion of inclusion and embracing the following ideas with ease.

1. I know I have biases, but it does not make me a bad person.
2. I understand that when I do not try to eliminate my biases, it can lead to prejudice both against some people and for other people as well.

3. I am aware there are many groups of cultures and different types of people in my organization. I want to know as much as I can about our differences so I can make them welcome and support their success in our organization.

Once these acknowledgements are made, we can move on to Disruption.

Step #2 – D for Disruption

I grew up in the Deep South, immersed in a culture where the LGBTQ community was strongly ostracized and condemned, forcing LGBTQ people to hide their true identities. Although I had friends from the LGBTQ community, I was criticized for those friendships and held conflicting feelings about them, an implicit bias I realized I had to face and overcome lest it hinder me as an inclusive leader.

Taking a course on managing diversity in LGBTQ communities allowed me to meet many members of that community and hear their stories. Doing so not only helped to dissolve my fears toward LGTBQ people, but it also helped me embrace and support them in ways that I had been unable to previously.

Understanding that I held this bias challenged me and forced me to put a plan into action to become more inclusive toward a particular group of people. Should you find yourself in a similar situation, you can move forward by recognizing which group you are biased toward, acknowledging your bias, and then learning as much about the group as possible. An implicit bias assessment can be a useful tool for getting started with identifying what our biases are and determining who they may affect within our workplace.

One of the most well-known tests is the Harvard Implicit Association test (IAT), a free online assessment that measures attitudes and beliefs that people may be unwilling or unable to report. For example, you may believe that Asian and American women are equally assertive when it comes to leading work teams, but the assessment could show that you (like many others) actually associate Asian women with being less assertive leaders than American women. The IAT asks 100 questions, provides clues on what biases you may have, and offers recommendations on how to overcome them.

The free online assessment unfortunately does not cover all possible areas of bias. Other implicit bias tests are much more detailed and costly – providing a more multi-dimensional analysis of what your implicit biases look like when comparing one diverse group to the other. For example, the assessment would indicate what your impressions are when comparing a wide range of diverse racial and ethnic groups and would also include groups of different sexual orientation, culture, nationality, language, dress and grooming style, age, and even cognitive and philosophical differences.

Because there may be a diverse collection of groups within your workplace, the more information you can gather and analyze about your biases, the better positioned you will be to become a more inclusive leader. An analysis of your results can show what behaviors need to change for you to become more inclusive and can guide you towards adopting up to five inclusive behaviors to implement over a specific period of time.

The High Cost of Failing to Disrupt Biases

Companies can suffer enormous financial losses or embarrassing press coverage when managers fail to disrupt their biases and continue discriminating against employees who belong to marginalized groups in the organization. A strong example of how things can go horribly wrong is what happened at FedEx with Jennifer Harris, an African American employee who was racially targeted by her boss. For 13 years, Jennifer worked at FedEx's corporate office. She had successfully risen in the company by outperforming most people in the sales division and winning numerous sales awards. After being promoted to an executive level position, however, her new supervisor began to make disparaging remarks – implying that she should return to her former position as an account executive. When Jennifer reported this to HR, her supervisor's behavior worsened, she was put on an improvement plan, and shortly thereafter, her employment was terminated. Jennifer enlisted a civil rights attorney and took FedEx to court, eventually winning a $366 million lawsuit. This type of incident is unfortunately not an outlier – many other billion-dollar companies whose efforts at inclusive leadership come up short are being hit with major racial harassment lawsuits.

Key Areas of Focus in the Workplace

One of the key areas to focus on as you work on becoming a more inclusive leader to the group you hold biases toward is the onboarding process, where you can work to become better attuned to the needs of each new person from that group as they are hired. Ensure they are assigned someone to guide them and answer questions about operations and processes as they settle into their new role. Next, ensure they receive clear and regular feedback about how they are doing, and ensure that other employees reach out to make them feel welcome. You should also work to ensure that team meetings are inclusive and that conversations are multi-directional so that any new person can offer useful input along with other staff members.

No matter who is being on-boarded, managers must ensure that everyone receives the same treatment – regardless of their cultural or ethnic background. An ideal way to determine if this is happening is to offer on boarded employees an anonymous survey within their first three to six months concerning what support and guidance they were given, and whether you and your team exhibited inclusive behaviors throughout their training and development process.

Step #3 – A for Adjust Our Alliances

After acknowledging and identifying your biases, and then taking steps to begin disrupting them, the next strategy is to become more cognizant of the various people in your workplace and move to develop alliances with employees with whom you have little or nothing in common. Typically, once people are on boarded and familiar with their coworkers they tend to stay in their comfort zones and build alliances only with people who look and act like them. As on reality television shows like Big Brother and Survivor, they play it safe, not going out of their way to befriend others who look different from them unless there is a direct benefit derived from it. Normally, Whites hang with Whites, Blacks with Blacks, LatinX with LatinX, Asians with Asians, and LGBTQ with LGBTQ.

These groups of cultural affinity are of some benefit – they enable employees to connect with others who share similar values and insights about the world. At the same time, however, workplace alliances should not hinder people from leaving their comfort zones and developing meaningful relationships with others from different places on the racial spectrum. Strategy #3 encourages people to be more inclusive while motivating them to become more culturally competent. By intentionally seeking out coworkers with whom to establish new relationships and alliances, they will move beyond being an ally in name only and focus on intentionally connecting and collaborating with others from different groups.

When we collaborate with someone whose culture we know little about, it triggers our natural human curiosity and puts us in a position to ask questions and independently explore their story. A great example of this is when I found myself working in Canada with Indigenous First Nations people for the first time. The stereotypes I held in my head about this cultural group – that they were minimally educated, overly shy, or temperamental and warrior-like – came from what I had seen as a child on TV dramas like Gunsmoke or Little House on the Prairie. When I finally got the chance to work with them, I discovered they were nothing like what I had envisioned. I realized that the stereotypes lodged in my brain were based on Hollywood propaganda that painted 'Indians' as bloodthirsty, illiterate, misguided souls who needed to be stripped of their sovereignty to allow Europeans to take over their land for humanitarian purposes.

Each new person I met in the organization differed widely from the next and I soon discovered that we shared more commonalities than differences. I had thought I would encounter older men in the top leadership positions, but the organization's CEO turned out to be female. My boss, who reported directly to the CEO, was also a woman – one who was much younger than me and as smart as a whip. Needless to say, as I adjusted what I knew of this cultural group, my long-held implicit biases began to disappear.

Working around others who belonged to a different cultural group allowed me to become intimately knowledgeable about a culture I had only seen on TV and read about in history books. It was eye opening to talk to someone from another culture and hear what they thought about themselves and the world around them, and at the same time, be able to ask them any question I wanted about their history, culture, and people.

As you stretch yourself it can end up being a win for you, for the new person you bond with, and for the organization in which you work. Imagine if everyone in every department of an organization decided to exit their comfort zones and develop new alliances within their department and other departments throughout the organization? Inter-departmental work arrangements could be formed and people from different cultural backgrounds could build strong alliances and grow in awareness of others who do not look or think like them. What if a Jewish person decided to do this with a Palestinian? Or what if this happened between Ukrainians and Russians, African Americans and Croatians, Atheists and Buddhists, Ethiopians and Eritreans? Encouraging employees to work together and build new, cross-cultural alliances is the key to developing and broadening the idea of inclusion within the organization.

Step #4 – Participate & Party

One of the biggest disappointments that minorities and employees coming from marginalized communities face after they have been on boarded is when they discover that potential opportunities for growth within the company may never materialize. When that happens, and they realize their day-to-day tasks are monotonous and boring, they soon look for greener pastures. Strategy #4 aims to disrupt that by kicking off the important work of mentoring – where the manager who strives to be inclusive looks for others to mentor, especially minorities who are newly on-boarded in the company. While it might be a stretch to take on more than one or two mentees, doing so will model the type of behavior you would like to see from others within the rest of the department. Other senior team members will soon follow in your footsteps and begin mentoring and training others whose cultural background or interests they do not share.

The P&P strategy disrupts the normal flow of relationship building and gets people used to working with those who look different from them, so everyone starts to see it as normal to associate and collaborate with others across different cultural spectrums. This will be a breath of fresh air for newcomers and employees from groups who have typically been left out of the flow of information, activities, and golden opportunities. It will also open up pathways of collaboration that can continue as people rise up in the organization.

Practically, this step can begin by getting people to take on work assignments together or stay in the same rooms when taking trips outside the city. While this cannot necessarily be mandated, people can be continually encouraged to go above and beyond with getting to know others who are different from themselves. You can also encourage interactions during non-official, after work social gatherings, though I typically recommend that people get to know each other in settings that are not loud and boisterous like nightclubs or restaurants where people have to raise their voices to be heard. More ideal settings are in coffee shops, at lunch counters, or even during an art gallery outing – anywhere a manager can get to know someone outside the workplace setting. Managers that are more ambitious may even go above and beyond and commit to serving within the larger community of a group with which they've struck up a special bond.

The P&P strategy starts you off with getting to know one or two people of different cultural backgrounds in your company to get to know more about their culture. At the same time, it opens the door for you to learn more and gain broader insights about their culture by committing to serve in the community. That could involve anything from serving at a food bank, volunteering in a local thrift store, or participating in a local arts festival to raise money for various underserved populations. Ultimately, this will be a win-win all the way around and strengthen the bonds of trust between you, the employee with whom you have developed the collaborative friendship, and the larger community as well. The real challenge of the P&P strategy is to remember it does not stop and start with one person or even with the community, that person is associated with. It should be ongoing and include different people from many different communities.

The larger benefit this could bring to your workplace is that it will help people shift their vision away from forming friendships only with people who look like them and shift their attention to setting new goals for reaching outside their own cultural group. Imagine for instance, if employees were asked to have lunch with someone they did not know from a community they did not know much about – and imagine if they received recognition on a quarterly basis for then reaching out to and serving in those communities. That kind of action could have the potential to shift how collaboration, inclusive interaction, and community service is practiced within your entire organization.

Last, but certainly not least, there is a big chance that the people who participate in these exercises will gain some insightful awareness and empathy for others who live in communities outside of their own.

Step #5 – Tackle and Take Down Strategy

The last strategy of the ADAPT model involves removing the vestiges of systemic racism from the workplace to make it more inclusive and welcoming for everyone. Though some employees may be uncomfortable even considering the idea that racism still exists within the organization, the point of this exercise is not to make everyone comfortable, but rather to adopt a 'what if?' mentality as you perform a careful review.

What if, for example, something is being said or done that is potentially racist, but no one has ever said anything about it? Because implicit biases are often hidden, some people may not recognize racist symbols in the workplace, or they may not perceive that a certain symbol may be harmful to someone from a different cultural background. The Confederate flag, for example, is a racist symbol that has been used to promote Southern pride and heritage. This flag has been displayed proudly by millions of White citizens in front of their public and private offices, at sporting events, and at every other type of major event imaginable, but it has never been a comfortable sight for African Americans, who view it as a symbol of hate harkening back to an era where it was okay to enslave people based on skin color. Many Whites did not hold that same perception and for them – as well as the many Blacks raised not to protest this symbol – it was difficult to understand why so many people wanted it removed from public places. It was only when the BLM movement became a champion against symbols like the Confederate flag, that momentum spiked, and most public Southern agencies decided to remove the image.

Similar opposition occurred towards old Confederate statutes throughout the south as young people began to realize that they were, in fact, symbols of hate whose existence had previously only been called into question by isolated groups of protestors – groups who would surround the statues and topple them to the ground amidst the wild cheering of onlookers from all walks of life. Until the rise of the BLM movement, no one had seriously challenged the legitimacy of these symbols, but once the practice of toppling grew increasingly common, political leaders were forced to protect the historical landmarks by removing them from public view and storing them in guarded warehouses. What had been seen as a one-off of political defiance eventually mushroomed and caught the attention of everyone. Southerners who had never thought of the Confederate flag and statues as symbols of fear that engendered disgust amongst people of color, were now being asked to deep dig and realize why so many people felt the way they did.

These are just two examples of what can happen in public and private workplaces when it comes to identifying what symbols may be offensive to those who do not share the same traditions as the dominant cultural group in the workplace. Unfortunately, there are other examples of racist practices that emerge at company parties, such as blackface, the custom where Whites color their faces black to imitate Black people while performing skits, singing songs, or even dressing like slaves and imitating how they would have talked back in the 1800s. While this might be considered humorous to Whites and other cultural groups unfamiliar with the history of slavery, the practice is highly insulting to Blacks and people of color.

Sometimes, blackface is even practiced at Halloween, with White people dressing up to imitate recording artists like Michael Jackson or Prince. This is the kind of blackface is not viewed as unfavorably because the artists are being admired rather than denigrated, but as a best practice, it is best to avoid in the workplace.

Any company that allows the use of blackface to demean cultural or racial groups, should discontinue the practice to ensure that no one is humiliated at the expense of others. This consideration should extend beyond Black-and-White stereotypes to include the full range of racial archetypes, including Middle Easterners being played as terrorist bombers, for example, or Mexicans as drug smugglers.

These are just a few examples of how stereotypes can be perpetuated in the workplace among minorities, making them feel both unwelcome and psychologically unsafe through exposure to toxic images and practices. The department manager may become aware of these toxic images and practices through observation – without being told directly by those offended – but fully rooting out all vestiges of systemic racism will take the eyes and ears of everyone in the workplace. In addition, in the same way that images or patterns of behavior can be objectionable, there are also remarks, jokes, and comments that need to be weeded out of the workplace. For instance, the practice of referring to new employees or interns as 'slaves' is the kind of thing that must be eliminated to ensure that no one is offended.

This strategy aims to level the playing field for everyone so that people no longer have to fear humiliation or victimization by actions that entertain a few at the expense of many. Changing the workplace to make it more inclusive can only happen when everyone can openly contribute to the discussion and rid the environment of what makes them uncomfortable. When something makes people cringe, they should be allowed – encouraged even – to raise their voices and speak their truth. The motto should be "Speaking your truth to bring about your peace."

How the ADAPT Model Can Bring About Positive Changes to Your Workplace

The effectiveness of the ADAPT model is only as strong as the number of people who participate in practicing its strategies collectively. The more involved, the stronger the overall return on investment (ROI) will be, because employees who adopt a collective goal tend to achieve greater outcomes. When the entire group joins in, a number of things happen. First, everyone becomes aware of both the urgency of the goal and its overall potential benefits for the team. Responding to a call to action that will improve things for the overall team tends to make people feel good about committing to a goal together. They also tend to hold each other accountable, making it more likely that they will complete the five strategies together.

Although the strategies are simple, managers and staff should understand that the process is more a marathon then a sprint and that no two people will have the same experience. By modelling the process of going through the five steps, managers can demonstrate that it is both doable and important for everyone to participate. The example they set will help employees see the exercises as worthy – making them more apt to join and complete the program.

It is typical for people to be concerned about completing their day-to-day before they fully invest time in a non-mandatory program, so managers will need to enlist assistance with coordinating all the moving parts and ensuring that everything is tracked efficiently. I do not recommend delegating the task of tracking all participation in the ADAPT program to the manager's administrative assistant, but rather to involve some of their direct reports or possibly bring in a point person to facilitate and oversee the trainings from the beginning.

Strategies 1 and 2, Acknowledge and Disrupt, can be done together and will likely take 4 hours or so to complete in total. The first piece of explaining how we are all programmed from a young age to internalize biases from our social upbringing can be accomplished with a PowerPoint presentation and then reinforced with exercises and examples showing how children are raised to think things that are literally untrue. It can be useful as well to have participants share about what they were taught while growing up that they have since learned to be untrue. Strategy 2, a straightforward implicit bias assessment, will then take 1.5 to 2 hours to complete, depending on how much time is needed to analyze and share the results.

It is ideal to follow the completion of Strategies 1 and 2 with a follow-up discussion to give an overview of implicit biases, show how they negatively impact work, and provide detail on how our biases show up in our actions and comments. This is an ideal time to link internal biases with microaggressions (MAs) so that employees begin to understand not only what MAs are, but how they show up at work, along with what things should not be said in meetings, in public or private discussions, or anywhere in the workplace at all.

Strategies 3 and 4, Adjusting Our Alliances and Participate & Party, are practical steps that can be introduced in one session. If a workplace is teeming with diversity, these steps will be less challenging to accomplish. But, if there are great numbers of employees who share the same cultural background and only a small percentage of people of color in the same department, it may be more challenging to afford the large number of employees an opportunity to develop alliances with so few. In such a case of disparate group sizes, it can be helpful to get creative with rotating group members into connection with each other or having the dominant cultural group reach out to form cross-cultural alliances in other departments. What is key is that everyone focuses on getting out of his or her comfort zones and building friendships with others who do not look like them.

This last exercise should be the capstone of the program where all the people in the workplace come together to discuss how to rid the department of any symbols or vestiges of systemic racism to make the workplace more inclusive, welcoming, and a place of belonging for all. This can involve bringing in an inspiring guest speaker and creating a celebratory atmosphere to represent the dawn of a new beginning in human relations for everyone in the workplace.

CHAPTER 4
WHAT IS IMPLICIT BIAS AND HOW TO IDENTIFY IT IN THE WORKPLACE

The first step in confronting prejudice involves knowing that most prejudice is learned at an early age. These early learnings become, for the most part, unconscious threads of thinking that sociologists call implicit bias, a term first coined in by psychologists Mahzarin Banaji and Anthony Greenwald in 1995. They argued that social behavior is largely influenced by unconscious associations and judgments. [7] While people do consciously express biases for or against certain things, the term implicit bias refers to bias that is hidden and largely unconscious.

The word "implicit" derives from French & Medieval Latin, and it means complicated, tangled, involved, and intricate – the opposite of "explicit," which means exposed, open, and transparent. When a person openly shares their prejudice against a certain group within society, it can be defined as overt racism, but when someone conceals biases against others – either unknowingly or unconsciously – it is best described as implicit bias.

Despite how open-minded most of us claim to be, we generally have a hard time accepting the fact that we carry around an invisible cloud of biases of which we are unaware. Even as a minority who had experienced discrimination while living and travelling around the world to places like Asia, Canada, and Africa, I carried biases that were difficult to flush out of my subconscious. For instance, because of how I was raised, I grew up to fear and frown upon people of the LGBTQ community – especially gay males – whether they were openly gay or closeted.

Although I would never intentionally discriminate against gay men or women, my discomfort with them led me to avoid them during my daily interactions as a student at Morehouse College – an all-male college I attended in Atlanta, Georgia in my youth. Like a lingering ghost, my LGBTQ bias followed me into social and workplace settings, despite my best efforts to not carry it forward. My bias persisted even as the LGBTQ movement began to gain socio-political influence in the U.S., during which time I remained unaware of how many people withheld the truth of their sexual identity from me. I hid behind the false rationale that people living a gay lifestyle were not entitled to the same legal protections as straight people. What I did not realize was that my prejudice was keeping me from developing meaningful relationships with gay people and the LGBTQ community both in and out of the workplace.

That all changed when I took a University of Texas at Austin course called Managing Diversity –one which I expected to focus on race and Black and White diversity. I was in for a big surprise. The very first night there was a panel discussion, and when I entered the room, I saw an all-White group of men and women sitting at the front of the class. The first panelist was a gorgeous White woman – she was so beautiful that I had difficulty taking my eyes off of her – she looked like a modern-day Elizabeth Taylor. I stared openly as I tried to figure out what she was doing as a guest in the class.

The instructor indicated that the evening's discussion would center on members of the LGBTQ communities, and the struggles they faced in the workplace. The Elizabeth Taylor-look alike – named Macy Torrance – opened the discussion by sharing that she had once been a happily married man. My jaw dropped as I listened to her describe feeling like a woman trapped inside a male body, forced to pretend that she was a man. I felt as though everything I thought I had known about transgender people had been instantly torn to shreds – I felt completely galvanized.

Macy – raised in a loving household as a boy named Matt Richardson – had always felt as though she was a woman in a man's body. Though she had pondered the idea of transforming into a woman, she had never gotten the support she needed from her family to make the leap. In adulthood, she married a woman whom she thought she was in love with, but her desire to become a woman eventually destroyed their bond. Macy decided that to find true happiness, she would need to undergo gender affirmation surgery. After extensive research, she opted to travel to Thailand because the procedure was much cheaper there than in the United States. After a successful surgery, Matt became the beautiful woman who I came to know as Macy.

Hearing about her amazing journey showed me what it really meant when someone said they felt they did not fit in the body they had been born into. It was at that point that I realized I could no longer hold onto my biases about other people's sexual orientations and identities. I needed to accept people unconditionally, no matter what. It was a mentally liberating experience and a catalyst for me to further examine my own implicit biases – especially with regard to how they affected me in the workplace.

How Implicit Bias Impacts You as a Leader

Recent studies have shown that the organizations with the greatest success rates embrace a diverse workforce and clientele, yet statistics show that most corporations, schools, and businesses still fail to do so. Why is that the case? In my work as a DEI trainer, I have come to see that one of the most crippling forces responsible for this failure is the very human characteristic of implicit bias.

We like to think of ourselves as free from prejudice, but really, no one is exempt. No one is free of implicit bias, regardless of their age, religious belief, race, gender, philosophical background, or upbringing. All humans – no matter where they are born or where they reside – are susceptible to the influence of the early prejudices they learn. To become an inclusive leader, managers must understand and confront implicit bias.

Implicit biases are *unconscious associations, beliefs, or attitudes towards social groups*. We all possess them – they come from our upbringing, culture, friends, media exposure, and from incidental interactions that result in the involuntary implanting of beliefs about groups of people. It may be helpful to think of implicit biases as erroneous instincts – default settings that exist outside your control because you simply do not know they are there. From an organizational point of view, implicit biases may lead to underestimating employees, misreading customers, overlooking talents in your workforce, or hiring and promoting the wrong people – things that may then result in workplace disparities, employee or client despair, organizational failure, and costly litigation.

Implicit Bias is Unconscious and Adversely Impacts the Workplace

It is important to recognize that implicit bias differs from explicit bias (one's conscious associations, beliefs, or attitudes toward social groups) and that a person's explicit and implicit biases may be at odds. A business executive may consciously believe in the inherent equality of the races, profess that belief, and make racial equity a stated goal in her organization, yet still hold unconscious racial beliefs that sabotage her leadership efforts and the success of her company. Any organization that values a diverse, equitable, and inclusive environment must work to educate its decision-makers about this phenomenon of implicit bias. The three main groups that can undermine a leader's efforts to become inclusive are Racial and Ethnic Biases, Gender Biases, and Sexual Orientation Biases.

Racial and Ethnic Biases

As a DEI practitioner, I see unconscious racial stereotypes and biases as a primary example of implicit bias. If the people who hold power in organizations show an automatic or subtle preference for one race or ethnic group over the other, this can be considered implicit bias. Not only does this type of racial and ethnic bias have a devastating effect on work relationships, it can carry broader legal implications if it is proven to be carried out regularly in small interpersonal interactions.

Examples of racial and ethnic bias may include associating Black individuals with violence. You may, for instance, cross the street when you see a Black man walking in your direction, without even realizing why you are doing so. Another typically held implicit stereotype is that Blacks are not as smart as Asians or Whites, and as a result, you may not assign Blacks or other visible minorities more challenging jobs in your workplace. As a result of a manager's implicit bias, he may compliment a Latino worker for speaking perfect English, assuming based on appearance that the worker is a non-native English speaker. When committed continually over time, these types of actions can be labeled as microaggressions – subtle, and often non-verbal practices that communicate a hostile, derogatory or negative prejudicial slight or insult toward any group.[8] In all these examples, implicit prejudice is exhibited without you even being aware of it.

Gender Biases

Another common major implicit bias that hurts inclusive leaders involves gender. Gender biases show up every day in our judgments of people based on traditionally assigned feminine and masculine traits. In the workplace, these typically show up when people in power discriminate against women and show favor towards men. An example of gender bias might be a manager passing over a women for a promotion to a sales manager position in favor of a man, despite her consistently outselling everyone in her department for the previous five years.

When women are held back from leadership roles because of company practices or because of someone's religious belief that women are inherently unequal to men, this is the very essence of gender bias. Unfortunately, gender bias is practiced at all levels of society, beginning in elementary schools where many teachers subconsciously believe girls to be inferior to boys in STEM fields (science, technology, engineering, and mathematics). As a direct result of this gender bias, girls are often relegated to nontechnical fields like languages and social studies. Practiced regularly in the workplace, gender bias can create a toxic and harmful work environment.

Sexual Orientation Bias

One of the least discussed biases that continues to plague a wide range of workplace environments is sexual orientation bias – or LGBTQ bias. A recent report from the UCLA School of Law called 'LGBT People's Experiences of Workplace Discrimination and Harassment', examined lifetime, five year, and past year of discrimination experienced by LGBTQ employees.[9] Some of its main highlights indicated that 46% of LGBTQ workers have experienced unfair treatment at work at some point in their lives. With over 8 million workers in the U.S. identifying as LGBTQ, discrimination and harassment against LGBTQ workers have been documented in a variety of sources and found to negatively impact employees' health and well-being and to reduce job commitment and satisfaction. The study further revealed that overall, 8.9% of employed LGBTQ people reported that they were fired or not hired because of their sexual orientation or gender identity in the past year, including 11.3% of LGBTQ employees of color and 6.5% of White LGBTQ employees. The percentage was five times higher for those who were out as LGBTQ to at least some people at work compared to those who were not (10.9 % compared to 2.2%).

Interestingly, the groundbreaking report also highlights how people's religious biases are a primary driver of their discrimination against LGBTQ workers. The report found that over half (57%) of LGBTQ employees who experienced discrimination or harassment at work reported that their employer or co-workers did or said something to indicate the unfair treatment was motivated by religious beliefs. Nearly two-thirds (63.5%) of LGBTQ employees of color said that religion was a motivating factor in the experiences of workplace discrimination compared to 49.4% of white LGBTQ workers.

One example of this type of religious implicit bias took place in Charlotte, North Carolina, when a gay substitute teacher was wrongfully fired by a Roman Catholic school after a 2014 social media post in which he announced plans to marry his longtime partner. In 2021, the U.S. District Judge Max Cogburn ruled that Charlotte Catholic High School and the Roman Catholic Archdiocese of Charlotte violated Lonnie Billard's federal protections against sex discrimination under Title VII of the Civil Rights Act.

McKinsey & Company reported recently in 'LGBTQ+ voices: Learning from lived experiences'[10], that coming out is especially challenging for junior employees, and that only one third of the LGBTQ+ respondents below the senior management level reported being out. Other findings indicated that women are far less likely than men to be out, and that only 58% of LGBTQ+ women – compared with 80% of LGBTQ+ men – said they are out with most colleagues.

The research indicates that LGBTQ bias is alive and well, and that it can have very cataclysmic consequences on organizations if it is left unchecked and not eradicated. One industry where this bias is especially pervasive is in public safety sector. In early 2023, the LA Times[11] reported a story that 12 Torrance police officers who took part in a racist text messaging scandal were no longer employed by the city. The text scandal was discovered in August 2021, when a Los Angeles County District Attorney filed vandalism and conspiracy charges against two officers who had allegedly painted a swastika inside a towed vehicle in January 2020. A search of the officers' phones showed that roughly a group of officers between 2018 and 2020 had allegedly exchanged 390 "anti-Semitic, racist, homophobic or transphobic remarks". The messages were rife with racial slurs and profane bragging about the use of violence against suspects. The messages also contained offensive remarks about Latinos, Jewish people, and members of the LGBTQ community. The scandal sparked an investigation by the California Attorney General's Office and a number of officers stepped down from the department. One of the officers who left complained openly about having to work with a gay colleague and, using an anti LGBTQ slur, vowed to punch that officer.

This persistence of such bias against LGBTQ employees demonstrates the importance of showing employees of all backgrounds how to be more inclusive – and most importantly – how to confront and eliminate their unconscious biases.

Implicit Bias and the Roots of Prejudicial Programming

Our parents, grandparents, and earlier ancestors held biases based on how they were indoctrinated in their homes, neighborhoods, schools, and nation-states. Though we may live in more culturally diverse nations today, that does not mean they are bias-free. In fact, the more different groups that exist in a nation, the more biased overall it tends to be, because there are more groups to hold biases against each other. In countries as large as the United States, Russia, and India, where population sizes range from three hundred million to one billion plus, the sheer number of racial and ethnic groups correspond to an equal level of biases held.

In the truest sense, organizations and companies are microcosms of our society, so it is only natural that implicit bias carries into the workplace. The prejudices that exist in our nation's myriad communities are also perfectly embedded in our companies – it is an unavoidable fact that people bring their biases to work with them. In fact, recent scientific studies have shown that biases are much like an iceberg, with the tip of the glacier representing our conscious knowledge – a mere fraction of all the things we know and feel. The unseen portion, below the tip of the iceberg, represents all of the unconscious feelings that form the biases we keep hidden and suppressed. In many instances, we remain unaware that we hold these biases unless we are confronted with evidence to prove they exist.

How Do We Come to Know What Our Own Biases Are?

Currently, there are several leading organizations studying implicit bias and finding ways to assess how they impact our lives as individuals and as social and organizational entities. Harvard University's assessment – the Implicit Association Test – can be found through their Project Implicit[12] website, and the following chapter will delve into how to use this assessment to discover and work towards eventually eliminating your own unconscious biases.

CHAPTER 5
HOW TO CONFRONT AND OVERCOME
UNCONSCIOUS BIASES

Perhaps the biggest challenge you will face in your role as a manager – besides trying to deal with your own biases – will be putting together a congruent strategy to combat the implicit bias being subtly practiced by all your employees. Even if you were to wave a magic wand and remove all of the biases from your own subconscious, it would still not prevent your team members from experiencing the negative effects of working in a non-inclusive workplace.

Now that we have an idea of what implicit bias is though, we can get started on the imperative work of implementing a step-by step strategy to move the team towards a bias-free work zone – one where people are treated equally and respected for the differences they bring to the organization. Once again, this is a good time to remember that reaching this goal will be a marathon, rather than a sprint. It will be an effort to accomplish and celebrate in stages over the next three to five years.

One of the first steps to overcoming workplace bias is to get your employees to understand what unconscious bias is, and how it can keep your company from reaching its full potential. While it might not be possible to accomplish this throughout the entire company, an aspiring inclusive leader must take it upon him or herself to get the ball rolling in the right direction. This entails taking the time to run workshops that teach team members about the hidden dangers of unconscious bias. No matter what an employee's educational or professional background, most of them are unaware of the hidden biases that exist in work environments. Moreover, in the same way that beachgoers do not understand the effects of hidden ocean pollutants, employees do not see how their biases can harm others in the workplace.

The sad truth is that no one wants to get vulnerable and admit they hold unconscious prejudices, which affect a company's results – so the issue is rarely discussed. In order to move out of a state of normative mediocrity, though, inclusive leaders will have to work hard to overcome pushback from those who think themselves free from unconscious bias and discriminatory practices. As you move into becoming an inclusive leader, there are several important steps you can take to usher your teammates down the path to change:

Keep DEI Alive in Your Monthly Meetings

Make time in your meetings to deal with DEI issues. Instead of quarterly discussions, be intentional about adding DEI to workplace meeting agendas once a month. During these discussions, make time to highlight not only the importance of diversity, equity, inclusion, but also the concept of belonging – giving space for every employee to offer input about how your workplace can become more inclusive for all. Even if there are currently no non-White employees in the room, the time to begin the discussion is now. This will ensure that when people of color are on boarded into the organization going forward, the shift in mindset will have already begun, with everyone already thinking about how the workplace will look and feel to someone new coming in.

Throughout my years working in managerial posts at various companies, I noticed that minorities tended to restrain their voices and not give input until asked. I came to see that it is very important to ensure that all of the people on the team are invited to share their feelings regardless of their rank or level of expertise. When I ran weekly meetings, I made sure to always scan the room to make sure that my employees of color felt both included and comfortable voicing their opinions about the topics on the table.

Unravel Unconscious Bias with the Harvard Implicit Bias Test

In laying out a plan to create a bias-free work zone, employees will also need to understand the types of biases that exist in the room, the division, and the overall organization. They must realize that no one is free from the influence of bias, whether they sit at the C-level or work in janitorial services. It should also be emphasized that the less bias there is, the more unified your workplace will be. You will need to explain all the different types of biases so that your employees do not maintain a narrow understanding. They must understand that workplace bias goes beyond color and race – it includes other biases around religion, nationality, age, gender, ethnicity, transsexuality, LGBTQ issues, and many more. Once you have shared this information with the group, you can move on to introduce them to the Harvard Implicit Bias Test assessment tool that can be found here: https://implicit.harvard.edu/implicit/takeatest.html

While taking the assessment may be an uncomfortable exercise for some of your employees, it is important for everyone on the team to realize that overcoming unconscious bias is a top priority, and that no one will be criticized and blamed for their assessment results. By using the online assessment, and answering its series of random questions, members of your team will discover where they land when it comes to unconscious biases. While the assessment is not 100% accurate, it will be useful for getting them thinking about their own biases – and it will give them a rough indication of what they need to work on. The free online assessment is a good place to start because the cost of more comprehensive assessments can run as high as $200 a person. Once everyone has their results, you can work with a facilitator to discuss the findings and summarize how biases can influence overall productivity in the organization.

As the manager overseeing these assessments, this is an opportunity to give your direct reports the support and resources they need to disrupt the biases they may be grappling with. I formerly worked with a public college in Northern California that lacked diversity in its executive leadership positions. They wanted to get ahead of the curve and learn how to deal with anti-black racism and discernable biases against other – mainly LatinX – minority employees. I recommended that they join The University of Southern California's (USC) online Race and Equity Center, which offers online training for overcoming organizational bias and racism in the workplace. After joining this educational collective, the college instituted the requirement that all employees attend monthly online sessions and report about the findings to the College's Board of Trustees. Each constituency in the College (management, faculty, classified staff) took turns sharing what they learned, and after a year, the College saw some very positive results. Before the meetings began, the entire executive and middle management team had consisted of only White employees. By the end of the year, however, the college had hired four new employees of color, two of whom served in key executive positions in the Department of Academic Affairs and Student Services. In retrospect, the College's $25,000 expenditure for joining USC's Educational

Collective, and the commitment made to enrolling all employees in its training, was undoubtedly a wise strategic investment – one that put the college on a path to becoming a more inclusive organization.

Hire a Facilitator to Lead the Process

As the manager in charge of this process, it will be important to get buy-in on developing a bias-free work zone. Rather than controlling the DEI dialogue yourself, though, you should consider having a facilitator lead the process. The main focus of these DEI discussions should lie in creating a vision of how the workplace will look, how the employees will engage with each other, and how you will create a place where everyone feels welcome. In these sessions, you will want to involve everyone in developing a mission statement, a set of values for each person to embrace, and a list of actions that will exemplify how each person will be there for each other. Every single one of your people will need to become an ally of everyone else in the workplace – and you and your team will need to work together to design exactly what that will look like.

Define What Biased Behavior Looks Like

Once that vision is clear, and you have a mission statement for how you will form a bias-free workplace, you can begin the work of teaching your employees how to confront and eliminate the effects of unconscious bias in the workplace. Merely writing the mission statement and setting the goals will not lead to the disappearance of biased behavior. You will need to hold ongoing training about what biased behavior looks like. Offer a workshop outlining what microaggressions are – unconscious words or behaviors that demean and humiliate others – so that employees are aware of what not to say or do towards their co-workers. You will need to explain and demonstrate how negative biases can harm company morale and negatively impact production and profits. As well, you will need to give your employees the tools for fighting bias in the workplace and make it clear that anyone committing these kinds of behaviors will be held accountable. Setting up an anonymous hotline for employees to use for reporting incidents of bias or racism in the workplace can be useful approach.

Overcome Affinity Bias in Hiring

One of the workplace areas most impacted by bias is in the hiring of new employees because of something called affinity bias; members of hiring committees inadvertently gravitate towards and end up hiring people similar to themselves. Left unchecked, this affinity bias ends up creating a decidedly non-diverse workplace. Employees must be educated on the harm that affinity bias can have on their organization. By providing them with training, you can help them become aware of how to hire based on the traits, skills and professional experience that will benefit your company. To create a diverse, inclusive, and successful workplace, new hires must be brought on based on who will be the best fit for the job. Some companies remove applicant names during the screening process to overcome affinity bias – forcing the screener to focus on skills rather than cultural differences.

Use Data to Determine If Your DEI Strategy Is Working

As an inclusive leader, you will also want to employ data to inform company decisions about how your inclusive workplace is continuing to evolve. Metrics to consider include: Are there more people of color working in your department than there were a year ago? Is there more or less conflict between employees compared to what there was a year ago? Perhaps most importantly, is there a newly formed, or growing sense of harmony in your workplace that could not be felt until recently? Is the DEI vision you and your team crafted coming to fruition, and if not, what needs to be done? Reviewing the data on an ongoing basis is a critical piece of your DEI strategy.

Raise the Voices of Minoritized Employees

Another crucial leg of the DEI journey is allowing people of color to be a key part of the diversity discussion. They should have a big voice in the matter and should be made to feel welcome to meet with managers and leaders to discuss progress – or lack thereof – and to speak honestly about any transgressions they witness being committed toward themselves or other people of color.

Assess DEI Goals in Annual Evaluations

Lastly, employees should be held accountable if they do not fulfill the goals you have set together for creating an inclusive workplace. As an inclusive leader, if you see evidence of discriminatory behavior, you must ensure immediate action is taken to protect the safety and wellbeing of those being affected.

As you move through these recommended steps for confronting bias in your workplace, realize that this is not something you can accomplish overnight. The key to achieving success lies in consistency. You will reach your goals by holding yourself accountable to including DEI trainings in your monthly meetings. You can also increase your chances of success if you designate a team of employees to assist with keeping the DEI vision and goals at the top of everyone's list of priorities. With the support of everyone, you and your team will be on your way to creating an inclusive workplace for all.

CHAPTER 6
WHAT WE CAN LEARN FROM COMPANIES THAT INCLUSIFY THEIR WORKPLACES

Until a few years ago, most companies prided themselves solely on whether they were considered a great place to work and whether they were profitable. Little attention was given to whether they had diversity in the workplace. When diversity was mentioned, it was primarily in the context of gender and race. However, in the post-George Floyd era, the issue of diversity and inclusion has come to the forefront, and it now covers a wide breadth of who we are as humans. We have come to see that diversity includes gender, race, ethnicity, religion, political beliefs, education, socio-economic backgrounds, sexual orientation, culture, and disabilities. Despite the fact that many organizations and their leaders are becoming more conscious of the benefits of a diverse work culture, there are still many that have no clue about the ostensible benefits of hiring people from a variety of different backgrounds. In this chapter, I will highlight several companies that are taking the lead in becoming more inclusive and also demonstrate how work-based DEI initiatives are creating real change in the lives of their employees. Conversely, I want to also shine a spotlight on companies that are not paying attention to the importance of driving this change and look at how that has a negative impact on their operations, their global reputations, and their bottom lines.

Cultural Change Brings Bias into the Spotlight

Two of the game-changing movements that have shed more light on systemic racial and gender bias in the workplace are the #BlackLivesMatter and #MeToo movements. Since their emergence, we have seen a significant increase in the number of workers speaking out against injustices – often by taking their employers to court about pay disparities, harassment and abuse, and toxic company culture. Some of the largest firms hit by lawsuits over allegations of racism and sexism include Google, Amazon, McDonald's, Pinterest, and Johnson & Johnson. In addition, although I am certain that each of these companies have divisions, subsidiaries, or franchises that do model inclusivity, I would bet that their inclusivity is hit and miss – that it does not run evenly throughout their organizations. Regardless of whether a company is profitable or has been deemed a great place to work, if it does not have systems in place to ensure the workplace is welcoming and infused with a sense of belonging, employees from a wide array of cultural backgrounds will continue to experience the humiliating and emotionally debilitating effects of racial and gender-based bias.

The Massive Costs of Harassment and Discrimination

It may come as a complete shock to many that some of the largest and most recognizable companies in the IT industry have been hit by multiple lawsuits alleging racial and sexual bias in their organizations, and that those patterns of abuse are systemic, rather than being isolated instances. We will examine lawsuits filed against the corporate behemoths by focusing on three companies – Amazon, Facebook, and Google. Let us begin with one of the largest fish in the proverbial corporate ocean.

In 2020, Amazon was hit with multiple lawsuits concerning questionable hiring practices involving women and people of color. One accuser – former hiring manager Lisa McCarrick – sued Amazon after her manager allegedly requested that she investigate social media accounts belonging to job applicants in order to determine their race and gender. When she complained that the practice was racially and sexually biased, she was terminated.

Later that same year Shaun Simmons, a transgender man, claimed in a lawsuit against Amazon that he faced harassment and retaliation while working at Amazon – being demoted and denied a promotion after telling his manager he was pregnant. Another lawsuit followed in November from Chris Smalls who alleged that Amazon's response to the pandemic was racially motivated – claiming the company violated civil rights laws by failing to protect Black, Brown, and immigrant warehouse workers from COVID-19, while at the same time looking out for its mostly White managers. These blatantly non-inclusive behaviors have not only made Amazon a target for future lawsuits, but the bad PR has turned job candidates away from applying for work at the company.[13]

Facebook was also forced to face the music when it was hit by multiple lawsuits. Numerous workers sued both Facebook and the Chan Zuckerberg Initiative – a private philanthropic organization run by Priscilla Chan and Mark Zuckerberg – over claims of racial bias. In their lawsuit, employees claimed that Black employees were underpaid, undervalued, and marginalized. In addition to that lawsuit, Facebook also came under Federal scrutiny due to a complaint that the company is biased against Black employees and prospective job candidates. This Federal investigation stemmed from a Facebook recruiter and two rejected job applicants filing a complaint with the Equal Employment Opportunity Commission accusing Facebook of "racial discrimination" against Black workers and applicants "in hiring, evaluations, promotions, and pay."

Another universally recognized company recently hit with lawsuits from both within and outside of their company is Google. Despite being one of the world's most profitable companies, it experienced an eruption of chaos in 2017 when four female ex-employees claimed that not only had they been underpaid by Google, but that the practice was widespread throughout the company. They alleged that women employed at Google are paid about $16,794 less than men in similar positions and asked the court to grant their lawsuit class action status, which would allow them to represent 10,800 other female Google employees. If the allegations prove to be true, Google's actions would indicate that some of our country's top corporate leaders allow a work environment which does not treat women equally and does not value their work at the same level as men. Google may ultimately have to pay out hundreds of millions of dollars to women who were wrongfully paid between $16,000 to $20,000 less than their male counterparts during years spent working for the company – compensation which will have to be dispensed retroactively.

What we can learn from these three examples is that despite being immense in size, highly profitable, and having worldwide success, companies can be brought down by a refusal to cultivate inclusivity, especially since the emergence of social media and the proliferation of smart phone use has made it much easier than it was ten to twenty years ago to prove that discrimination and bias exists.

Big Name DEI Leaders

Thankfully, there are companies and corporate leaders working on paradigm shifts and attempting to do the right thing by developing inclusive work environments which treat a diverse workforce with equity and mutual respect. Three companies making big strides towards making inclusivity central to their operations and branding include the Dallas Mavericks – an NBA Franchise led by billionaire Mark Cuban, Fenty – a dynamic cosmetic company under the creative leadership of Rihanna, and Starbucks – a multi-billion-dollar coffee dynasty led by CEO Howard Schultz. There are many others who are also working to be inclusive, but we will focus on these three in particular to show how their efforts are working in their employees' favor and, in turn, helping them to grow and prosper.

The Dallas Mavericks – one of the top NBA sports franchises in the country – is valued at over $3.5 billion dollars. Mark Cuban purchased the company in 2000, and after he ran it for almost two decades, it was found to have 20+ years of sexual harassment and workplace misconduct issues. The results of a seven-month-long investigation confirmed that the sports franchise had committed sexual harassment and workplace misconduct – evidence that was exposed in 215 interview with the current and former employees. In the end, the debacle cost Mark Cuban over $10 million dollars, which he contributed to women's causes. To his credit, Cuban decided to face the problem head on, and he began searching for candidates whom he felt could bring unity to his organization. He wanted a leader who would treat women and minorities equitably and support them in an organization that had been run predominantly by White males.

To change the culture, make a difference in the lives of his employees, and eliminate his organization's hostile work environment, Cuban had to think and dream big. Ultimately, he took the bold step of making Cynt Marshall the first Black female CEO to run an NBA sports franchise. Since taking the helm, Marshall has focused on hiring a diverse executive team. When she started, there were no women or people of color on the Mavericks' leadership team.[14] Today, 50% of all employees are women and 47% are people of color. She also brought an authentic leadership style to the Mavericks. When her tenure began, one of the first things she did was hold one-on-ones with employees to learn about their lives. She wanted to know about everything from childhood right up to adulthood, not just about their career aspirations. According to Marshall, Cuban wasn't necessarily looking for a woman or a person of color. "He didn't care. I often say, 'Mark was not trying to make history. He was trying to make a difference for his employees." Cuban says he hired Marshall "because she is amazing, forceful, dynamic, nurturing."

Starbucks is another company that is very intentional about creating inclusivity on their teams and in their stores throughout the world. Although they have faced a fair share of allegations of racial and sexual bias – from both employees and customers

– they have found proactive ways to handle these incidents and show that they genuinely care about treating others with equity. One incident that received major attention took place at a Philadelphia store location when two Black men waiting to meet someone for business purposes were asked to leave; the store manager called 911 and the pair was arrested for allegedly trespassing. After this dreadful incident, the CEO of Starbucks apologized directly to the two men for their experience of being racially profiled. Chairman Howard Schultz decided that under no circumstances could he allow the same thing to happen again. He made the bold decision to do a one-day anti-bias training across 8000 of their stores. By all estimates, Starbucks lost $16 million in sales revenue that day – June 11th, 2018 – but Schultz countered that maintaining the status quo would have been much more costly. What became readily evident was that Starbucks leaders were entirely committed to ensuring that inclusion and diversity initiatives were kick started with true purpose.

As of October 3, 2021, the Starbucks U.S. partner (employee) base was 71.3% female and 48.2% Black, Indigenous, and People of Color (BIPOC). Breaking down that BIPOC representation further, their partners are 7.7% Black, 28.5% Hispanic or Latinx, 5.9% Asian, 4.8% two or More Races, 0.6% American Indian or Alaskan Native and 0.5% Native Hawaiian or Other Pacific Islander. The company has also committed themselves to making the D&I process transparent by tying all executive compensation to building inclusive work settings, increasing spending with diverse suppliers from $794 million in 2021 to $1.5 billion by 2030, and growing small business investments in communities of color from $20 million in 2021 to $100 million by 2025.[15] While the company may have made some missteps along the way to becoming more inclusive, these initiatives show that Starbucks is putting its money where its mouth is.

In one last example, we look to an up-and-coming company called Fenty, which was launched by pop singer Rihanna in late 2017. Now a billionaire from building a global fashion empire, Rihanna is – probably more than anyone else in the fashion industry – pushing to normalize diversity in how she produces, markets, and brings her products to the world.

The fashion and beauty care industry has not always been at the forefront of inclusion. By and large, non-White consumers have had difficulty using products that were developed for and marketed to White women. Rihanna's goal with starting Fenty Beauty was to create a product line which included 40 different shades of foundation that could be adapted to all types of skin. In 2020, she went a step further with Savage x Fenty – a fashion show which premiered on Amazon Prime – in which she cast models of every gender, skin color, and body shape. The show was enormously successful and won critical acclaim for its capacity to highlight and normalize diversity. Providing that kind of high-profile platform for all different types of models promotes diversity across the entire fashion industry.[16] Under Rihanna's leadership, Fenty has become one of the fastest growing cosmetic companies in the world, being named to Time magazine's list of 25 best inventions of 2017, alongside NASA's Martian spacecraft Insight, Apple's iPhone, Nike's Pro Hijab, and the Tesla Model 3.

When organizations reframe their purpose and solidify a mission to become inclusive, they invest in helping employees feel comfortable about their own differences. In turn, this supports employees in learning and caring about others who may not share the same cultural, ethnic, or social characteristics as them.

CHAPTER 7
THE FIRE BREATHING DRAGONS THAT UNDERMINE INCLUSIVE WORKPLACES

Unless we consciously work to make our ethnically shifting workplaces more inclusive and welcoming, our employees will resist building relationships with coworkers who don't look like them, or who they don't relate to culturally and otherwise. We must intentionally commit to building a solid foundation of belonging and inclusion. To do so, we must stamp out the actions and mindsets I refer to as 'The Four Fire Dragons' of discrimination.

The Four Fire Dragons

Fire Dragon # 1 - Cultural Assimilation

Erroneous ideas regarding cultural assimilation are undermining workplace inclusion. When members of the workplace majority expect new employees from different cultures to culturally assimilate – adopt the same appearance, dress, speech, and behavior as the majority – it creates tension and anxiety for the visible minorities who feel they cannot be their authentic selves.

For centuries, non-White communities were forced to adopt the attitudes, social customs, and fashion choices of the dominant group. In the case of dress and grooming policies, for example, many companies still consider dreadlocks, braids, and natural hairstyles like an afro, to be outside the mainstream, and therefore want them banned. However, in order to become inclusive, companies will need to shift their perspective away from antiquated grooming policies from the 20th century, and instead focus on individual performance.

Over the years, various cultural movements have demanded that employees be allowed to retain their cultural customs without fear of reprisal. Currently, the Equal Employment Opportunity Commission, (EEOC) has multiple lawsuits pending against companies that have violated people's rights over hairstyles. In one such case, a woman named Chastity Jones was interviewed by Catastrophe Management Solutions (CMS) in Mobile, Alabama. According to Jones, a White human resources manager took issue with her dreadlocks, saying the style was against company policy because dreadlocks "tend to get messy, although I'm not saying yours are, but you know what I'm talking about." Jones went to the EEOC, and in 2013, they filed a lawsuit on her behalf, citing Title VII of the Civil Rights Act of 1964. Despite the fact that on September 15, 2016 the U.S. Court of Appeals ruled in favor of CMS' decision to refuse to hire Jones because of her dreadlocks, there has been a growing legal push to overturn this ruling at the state level.[17]

For instance, in the state of California, Governor Newson signed a bill into law in 2019 that protects people in workplaces and K12 public schools from discrimination based on their natural hair. The new law – known as the Crown Act – became the first of its kind to prohibit the enforcement of grooming policies that disproportionately affect people of color, particularly black people. It includes bans on certain styles, such as Afros, braids, twists, cornrows, and dreadlocks (locks for short). Newsom affirmed that the need for the protection of people's hairstyles had entered the national political consciousness in December of 2018 when a referee forced a black wrestler for a New Jersey high school to cut his dreadlocks or forfeit his match. That indignity forced the student to choose whether to "lose an athletic competition or lose his identity," Newsom said.[18]

Other examples cultural assimilations can include:

- Embracing the language of the prevailing culture as a primary mode of communication.
- Alteration of one's name to a more "Western" equivalent.
- Discarding traditional fashion choices and clothing in preference for the fashion of the dominant culture.

- Intentionally disregarding the education and credentials you received in your home culture due to the belief they no longer have worth to you.
- Participation in the holidays and celebrations of the dominant culture.
- Conforming one's accent or dialect to the speech patterns of the dominant culture.
- Internalization of the values and beliefs of the dominant culture.
- Disavowal of one's cultural heritage or identity.
- Abandonment of traditional spiritual practices and beliefs.
- Adopting the relationship expectations and dating norms of the dominant culture.

Fire Dragon # 2 - Unconscious Bias Against People of Color

Fire Dragon #2 raises its head whenever a manager believes visible minorities to be inherently inferior to White employees and limits them to roles that are less challenging or impactful as a result. This can destroy a sense of trust among employees over time, and it often leads to lawsuits as well. Though the manager may not be aware of their unconscious beliefs, it will insidiously seep into their actions, and cause them to favor those employees who look like them. I honestly believe that most managers do not intend to undermine employees of color, but unfortunately, there are some who unknowingly commit discriminatory acts because of the biases they learned at an early age and continue to harbor into adulthood. It is not enough for managers and leaders to believe that they treat everyone equally – they have to be aware and readily mindful of their biases with the understanding that becoming an inclusive leader is a lifelong process. Some of the common types of biases that show up when leaders interact with employees of color are the following:

Affinity (like-me) Bias: The unconscious tendency to better get along with, or give higher ratings to, people who are most like you.

Power Bias: Where you tend to rate, yourself higher than you do other people based on cultural or ethnic differences. As a person's power increases, so does their tendency for power bias.

Implicit person theory/ Personal growth mindset: If you don't believe that people can change – and therefore have a fixed idea of what their ratings should be – you exhibit this bias.

Recency bias: Where you focus only on more recent events and ignore an employee's performance over the entire review period.

Primacy bias: When leaders allow their first/early impressions to affect how they view an employee.

When these biases become manifest in the workplace and are not disrupted or acknowledged by the leaders who lead diverse teams, these types of actions adversely affect the morale, productivity, engagement, and retention of employees in the company.

While most people do not consciously feel superior to others who are different from them, their unconscious feelings of superiority – if not addressed upfront – will, over time, expose the biases that lie dormant in the recesses of their psyche. As Gundling and Williams argue in their book, *Inclusive Impact: Global Impact*, inclusion efforts must address deep-rooted issues of interpersonal and institutionalized racism. They argue that managers cannot easily gloss over these issues and that minority employees want to have a 'seat at the table,' and a real voice in discussions, decision-making, and changes in organizational processes and systems to ensure greater workforce equity.[19]

Fire Dragon # 3 - Unfair Treatment Towards People of Color

Fire Dragon #3 – the unfair treatment towards employees of color – is equally harmful to efforts to build inclusivity. This is when unconscious bias toward a particular group of people manifests as a negative action, or through insults, indignities, or slight put-

downs. These types of verbal slights are known as microaggressions. While microaggressions can sometimes be viewed as innocent or harmless, they actually reinforce stereotypes and are a form of discrimination. For example, if you are a male running a meeting, and you ask a female team member to take notes because you believe women to be better note takers than men, you are making an assumption based on a stereotype. It is no different than asking an Asian member of the team to complete a task requiring extensive math because you believe they will be great at it because of their Asian background. Many times, people make statements like these without being aware that they are committing microaggressions.

As a man and a person of color, I have experienced microaggressions all through my career – from supervisors, senior leaders, and even mentors. I have been complimented by leaders who were surprised that I could finish my projects on time along with my White colleagues, implying that, more often than not, Black employees cannot complete their assignments on time and responsibly. In other situations, I have been the only Black member of an executive team, and no matter what I recommended, people acted as if I were invisible. These microaggressions made me feel undervalued and resentful that I was not respected and better utilized. Other examples of microaggressions that have been aimed at people of color and marginalized populations include the following:

Asking a non-white person "Where are you from?" or "Where are you really from?" Such questions assume that someone who is non-White must be from somewhere else, implying that only White people are true Americans.

Telling an LatinX employee that they speak English very well or assuming that they were born overseas. These types of compliments indicate that you're surprised someone who isn't White can be intelligent and that most people who look like them aren't intelligent.

Saying to someone who is LGBTQ, "You don't look gay." This comment is an insult to LGBTQ people, and implies that their sexual orientation is not valued and should be overlooked.

Asking a Black person if you can touch their hair or whether it is real. This comment is especially insulting if it is aimed a black or brown woman employee.

To be an effective leader, it is imperative that you remain aware of the harmful impact that microaggressions can potentially have in the workplace and be ready to use your influence to share this information with the members of your immediate team.

Fire Dragon # 4 - Lack of Advancement of Minority Employees

The fourth Fire Dragon shows up when managers deliberately neglect considering visible minorities for career advancement opportunities because of the unspoken notion that people of color don't meet the success criteria typically embraced in corporate circles. While this kind of treatment is more subtle and nuanced than other discriminatory practices, people are not keenly aware of it when it does occur. The fact is, minorities are twice as likely not to be promoted as their white counterparts are, and inclusive leaders should take it upon themselves to go against the grain and be proactive in developing, coaching, and promoting diverse talent. Without a doubt, this is one of the important steps to building trust among diverse teams and ensuring all members can reach their fullest potential.

Slaying the Four Fire Dragons

Organizational leaders should understand that developing inclusive learning environments starts with a global strategy.

They must commit to establishing resources for all workplaces and divisions to work together towards inclusivity based on the same mindset and vision. If only one or two environments in the organization are inclusive and the rest are not, it will not foster unity for the whole. Unless leaders require all managers and staff to replicate patterns of inclusion in all their workplaces and environments, the inclusion and equity goals will be seen as optional and unimportant across the board.

I can say that 90% of the time, when managers opt not to make inclusion a top departmental priority, they ultimately maintain the status quo of treating people – especially diverse employees or students – in inequitable and socially unjust ways. When this hits a tipping point, one of the first negative boomerangs is for people who have been treated unequally to file grievances, which later turn into lawsuits. It takes time for this to play out, and in the end, most managers end up denying that a problem ever existed and stubbornly support the bad actors who caused the mistreatment instead.

Matters like these often end up either being brought before a judge or resolved out of court; either way, the organization ends up facing negative PR from the public airing of nasty details between the employee filing the lawsuit and the suspect who caused the grievance. This engenders distrust amongst those working within the organization, as well as the general public and the organization's customers as well. Usually, when this kind of abuse occurs in one part of the company, it is present in many others – with people turning a blind eye towards the mistreatment of those affected.

Inspiring organizations to transform their leadership from good to great takes work. The steps that follow will help you transform into an inclusive leader and move towards getting everyone on your team to follow. All it takes is for one person to lead the way so the rest can follow suit!

Moving Past Obstacles as an Aspiring Inclusive Leader

In the same way that you can feel positive energy when you walk into an office or retail space, negative energy can be perceived when inclusive behaviors are not being manifested by the employees in the organization. Some people may think that inclusive work environments evolve on their own into happy pockets of multiculturalism, but in reality, it takes a lot of intentionality and hard work. Inclusive work environments do not manifest by chance, and they do not arise out of the efforts of any single person.

There are rare leaders who are able to create inclusive work environments and generate a sense of belonging and security for all employees regardless of their differences. They do whatever it takes to positively engage and interact with their diverse team of employees who hail from a wide range of cultural and ethnic backgrounds. The four criteria that constitute the hallmark of such an inclusive leader include the following:

1. Building positive relationships with everyone in the organization

Inclusive leaders work to build bonds of unity wherever they tread in an organization. Ideally, they build their strongest bonds in the departments or divisions they lead, but they also leverage building relationships with people in other departments and leaders higher up in the organization. Wherever they go, and no matter who they meet, their goal is to build on these organizational connections with the understanding that each person is important in the grand scheme of working towards workplace inclusivity.

2. Cultivating a sense of belonging in his/ her workspace for everyone on the team

To an inclusive leader, everyone on the team is like family. Although members of the team come from a wide range of cultural and ethnic backgrounds, an inclusive leader respects and embraces all aspects of their diversity, realizing that each member brings special talents and gifts to the organization. Making all team members feel welcome engages them. The inclusive leader also puts team members at ease, which leads them to freely express ideas and share contributions which positively impact the organization.

3. Making sure that he/she is committed to everyone's success

Inclusive leaders are committed to supporting the success of every person on their team – no matter how different they may be. Even when things go wrong with employees, they take the time to listen. Inclusive leaders find ways to support employees who may not fit in, or those who, for whatever reason, want to leave the organization. For example, when I worked for Colorado Mountain College, I was the only African American employed on their 9,000 square mile, 11-campus College. Despite the pushback I received from some faculty members who claimed I was not the right fit and did not understand their 'Rocky Mountain' culture, the college Chancellor at the time went against the grain and supported me (much to the chagrin of some faculty and staff leaders). When my campus President found another job, instead of giving the interim position to someone who looked like him, he chose me.

When this was announced on the local paper's front page, there was a huge uproar. I felt firmly validated as an employee – despite many people being upset and working to undermine me. It motivated me to work longer hours and work harder to make that college a better place for all students. Those college leaders offered everyone a shining example of inclusive leadership. They did what true inclusive leaders do: lift up each employee – to the benefit of the workplace as a whole.

4. Treating all people equally

Inclusive leaders must treat everyone equally – no matter how they feel about their cultural or ethnic differences – in an effort to keep equity at the core of all workplace decisions. The inclusive leader focuses on keeping the process of building inclusivity transparent while carefully considering how each decision impacts everyone in the group. The awareness that their actions are being closely scrutinized will force aspiring inclusive leaders to think twice before doing things that favor those with whom they share the same cultural identity. When decisions involving the allocation of money, resources, appointments, assignments, and advancements are made, inclusive leaders will understand the negative impact a decision can make when it is not based on social justice. In the past it may have seemed that leaders could make discrete decisions – without the fear of any wide-reaching reactions or repercussions. In the age of social media, however, that has all changed.

Consequences of not investing in inclusive leadership in the age of social media

The explosion of recent technological developments has accelerated our ability to share information online with anyone anywhere in the world within seconds. Secrets formerly kept hidden behind closed doors regarding disputes, interpersonal conflicts, confrontations – and even just casual public observations – can now be recorded and shared with millions across social media platforms in the blink of the eye. Platforms like Facebook, Google, LinkedIn, Twitter, Snapchat, TikTok and Instagram are turning our world upside down and making our workplaces more transparent than ever. Instead of Big Brother watching us, we now have the power to not only watch Big Brother, but also to hold him accountable for workplace inequities.

Social media has given individuals the power and courage to stand up to our modern-day industry Goliaths. One such example occurred recently when a long-term employee of Starbucks was let go because he had closed the store early. Josh, who had been a Starbucks barista for 20 years, informed his crew of nine team members that he had been fired, and every single one of them resigned in protest, taking a group photo and posting it online. Over 26 million readers viewed their post within 24 hours, and it came out that Josh was fired not because he had closed the store early, but rather because of rumors that he had pushed to unionize his store, something Starbucks staunchly opposed. The company had not met with him to verify or discuss the rumor, and when he received his layoff notice, he was told to leave the store, and he was not offered severance pay or even a last bag of free Starbucks coffee.

If this had happened 20 years ago it would have gone unnoticed by the world. Today, regardless of how powerless retail or office workers are, they can lift their phones and record events in real time, turning into modern-day Walter Cronkite's reporting on workplace injustices. This is a wake-up call for companies that have until now failed to treat their employees equitably. Starbucks is just one company of the thousands that have been smacked by the power of social media. Though not without its drawbacks, social media helps expose the inconsistencies dwelling under the cloak of corporate social responsibility – and that is an important weapon in the fight for inclusion. Despite organizations widely promoting in marketing campaigns that they practice equity and inclusion, the statistics reveal the opposite to be true. American companies have miles to go before reaching the mountaintop of justice that Dr. King mentioned in his speeches some 40 years ago. Now that organizational malfeasance can be shared with thousands of groups and individuals at the press of a button, inclusive managers should do their due diligence to ensure all are treated equally.

CHAPTER 8
HOW TO GROW AND MEASURE
INCLUSION IN YOUR ORGANIZATION

As a Black man working in corporate America, I rarely felt that the bosses I reported to have my back, and since I was the only person of color in the organization most of the time, I always felt like the odd man out. In one-on-on meetings with my bosses, either I was spoken down to or had my ideas belittled and downplayed as insignificant – to the point that I stopped sharing my ideas in order to avoid the putdowns. What I had to do was get buy-in from other colleagues or community leaders before I approached my boss about anything, knowing that once he or she saw a strong level of support coming from other managers or peers, it would be hard for them to tell me 'No'.

I remember when I was hired to be an executive leader at a college in California – the President told me that he was bringing me on to run Student Services, and that he wanted to use my expertise to build learning communities on campus. Once I was hired, however, he shot down every proposal I made to him and did not let me implement anything in my first year in the position. Not only that, he did not want me to leave the campus to pursue professional development; after 12 months, I wanted to quit. I became depressed as a result of the subtle pushback I got from him. I noticed that he treated the other Vice Presidents – who happened to be White – respectfully, but he challenged me in meetings and talked down to me. I stayed in the position because I had no other job to pivot to, but I was miserable to the point that I did not want to go to work anymore.

As the only African American in the organization, I felt trapped. I was afraid if I called my boss out, I would be let go. I also felt I could not approach the HR rep because she was very close to the President and rumor had it that she had previously leaked information about confidential discussions to him. I came to feel like he had only hired me because he had to, and that he had put me on the shelf to die. After a year I felt like I was dying on the inside, with no one to take my predicament to – not to him, not to my all-White staff, not to HR, not the Board, not even to a lawyer. Because I had a family to support, I was forced to hold onto the problem – which, metaphorically, was like hot molten iron – and pray that it would not burn through my flesh. I think this is how many minorities cope with working in non-inclusive work environments. They just hold on to the hot molten iron, keep a smile on their faces, suffer in silence, and hope that things will get better.

Companies often pride themselves on the number of people of color they have hired and on boarded from one year to the next, but it is rare to hear them speak about how these employees are doing emotionally, what struggles they may be facing, and how they are being supported so that they can excel in their jobs. While measuring the growth of diversity among your employees is very clear-cut from a numerical standpoint, using metrics to measure inclusion is much more challenging. It has to be gauged from what your employees reveal to you about their experiences and perceptions tied to equity and their sense of belonging in the workplace. Aside from growing inclusion, one of your key responsibilities as an aspiring inclusive leader will be to have clear guidelines and criteria for measuring its impact in your workplace from year to year.

If managers want to ensure that their workers do not go through the type of ordeal that I experienced in my VP role, their first step in measuring inclusion has to begin with being intentional on developing the six signature traits of inclusive leaders that were covered in chapter two. Learning these leadership traits should not be assigned solely to those in the C-suite, or even to just a few people in middle management. This process should include every manager, assistant manager, and team leader in the department. Anyone and everyone who is interested in making inclusion sustainable in the organization should be provided with the necessary tools and educational training to make it happen.

Again, the six Cs of inclusive leadership include the following traits:

Commitment: Inclusive leaders make DEI a top priority and bring their A-game to the office every single day of the week.

Courage: Inclusive leaders realize that DEI work is hard, that they do not have all the answers, that they will make mistakes, and that this is a marathon, not a sprint.

Cognizance of Bias: Inclusive leaders realize that they have bias and must develop a sense of humility when learning about other people's social and cultural backgrounds.

Curiosity: Inclusive leaders need to be curious about other people's differences and try to understand the world and other cultures, while seeing learning as a lifelong process.

Cultural Intelligence: Inclusive leaders gather information that will make them aware of others who differ from them culturally and socially and help them interact in a way which produces positive results in and out of the workplace.

Collaboration: Inclusive leaders are plugged into the idea of being able to work with others harmoniously, and not letting cultural differences get in the way of forging positive relationships that can evolve into long-lasting friendships.

Tools for Growing and Measuring Inclusion

Providing ongoing training for your staff is key to informing and enlightening your team about what it takes to develop an inclusive work environment. To determine if your training programs are helping to build inclusion, your staff will also need to be surveyed and asked what they think about the overall process. Direct employee feedback can be a great way to gather information – both in the beginning to find out what the workplace needs are, and later on as a follow-up to determine how effective the trainings have been. It can be helpful to begin with some base dimensions for measurement.

The multinational research and consulting firm Gartner interviewed 30 DEI executives and reviewed extensive academic literature to identify key dimensions of inclusion. They then created 45 statements related to those dimensions and surveyed nearly 10,000 employees worldwide, rating the employees' level of agreement with each statement. According to Gartner, the more employees agree with the seven statements below, the more inclusive an organization is:

1. **Fair Treatment**: Employees at my organization who help the organization achieve its strategic objectives are rewarded and recognized fairly.

2. **Integrated differences:** Employees at my organization respect and value each other's opinions.

3. **Decision Making:** Members of my team fairly consider ideas and suggestions offered by other team members.

4. **Psychological Safety:** I feel welcome to express my true feelings at work.

5. **Trust**: Communication we receive from the organization is honest and open.

6. **Belonging:** People in my organization care about me.

7. **Diversity**: Managers at my organization are as diverse as the broader workforce.

By using the seven metrics above, inclusive leaders can survey their staff on a regular basis to find out what progress is being made, gauge where the weak points are, and figure out where there needs to be more support and training.[20]

Focus Groups

Another way to determine if inclusion goals are being met is to hold focus groups. Rather than relying on surveys – which are done in private with no face-to-face exchange of authentic discourse – people can be invited to affinity focus groups based on their cultural or ethnic identities. Gathering people in these types of groups can help them feel more open to sharing what is happening to them – because they end up being able to speak up as a group, rather than having to come forward alone as an individual voice. As an example, the following questions can be asked:

1. What does your direct manager say or do that makes you feel valued and respected? In what ways does his/her behavior make you feel the opposite?
2. Tell me about a time when "being different" from others at work affected your willingness to share an opinion or idea.
3. What can the organization do to make you feel a higher sense of belonging?
4. How does your organization foster an environment where people who come from different backgrounds know that their ideas are valued? Where does it fall short? What specific actions would make it better?

Focus groups are not without their drawbacks – holding focus group meetings across an entire company may sometimes end up being costly and time-consuming, especially in large organizations. Or, if you don't have a moderate number of employees of color, it might be difficult to assess what the real needs are, but you can get started with those people who are interested in participating, get the ball rolling, and continue to hold the meetings from year to year. You will need to determine what model is right for your organization's size and level of diversity and adjust on an ongoing basis.

Conduct Surveys

Many organizations conduct company-wide engagement surveys every one or two years, but in order to determine if DEI goals are being met, a survey needs to be done twice yearly. To identify what people are experiencing based on their racial or ethnic identities; they may prefer to complete the survey anonymously, out of fear that they may be targeted for their authenticity in answering the questions. Analyzing the answers through the lens of race, color, ethnicity – and the other wide spectrum of differences – will help you identify themes and patterns in the way the questions are answered. By comparing the responses of specific groups of employees – men versus women, managers versus non-managers, newcomers versus veteran employees, Blacks vs. Whites, LatinX vs Asian – companies can identify highly inclusive teams or business units, as well as trouble spots. These insights can then shape future priorities for research, training, and intervention. Companies can also develop original survey questions based on the qualitative data they glean from focus groups.

No matter how they choose to measure inclusion, what matters most is that DEI leaders ask for feedback from all their team members. Moreover, knowing how sensitive this information gathering can be, they must be patient and understanding, realizing that not all participants will feel safe, and that some may even feel threatened that confidential information could be misused or disclosed to their managers or colleagues. Nonetheless, in order for inclusion to be measured, employees will need to share their perceptions about relationships with their coworkers and leadership team, while also analyzing the team's culture, policies, and practices. For companies to successfully create a consistent scorecard for inclusion, they must ensure that the identities of all employees who participate in the surveys are protected, and that whatever information they share cannot be used against them.

CHAPTER 9
CHARTING THE COURSE – STAYING ACCOUNTABLE TO ACHIEVING INCLUSIVITY

Being the Proverbial Quarterback of Your Workplace

As an inclusive leader, you play a key role in guiding your team's actions toward scoring organizational goals on a daily, weekly, and annual basis. While it may be a stretch to compare you to an NFL quarterback, there are some similarities between your role and what an NFL quarterback is required to do. In the same way that a QB has to coordinate plays and lead the entire team down the field to consistently score and (hopefully) win games, organizational leaders are expected to inspire their team members to work efficiently together to win with their KPIs (key performance indicators).

However, while a QB's responsibility lies in outperforming another team within a 4-hour window once a week, organizational leaders must lead their teams five days a week, from 8 a.m. to 5 p.m. For them, game day is every day, not just on Sunday, leaving them with little time to rest and recuperate. And, because they plan day in and day out, it is crucial for inclusive leaders to see the game as a marathon run, rather than a quick sprint down the field. While NFL quarterbacks are under more intense pressure to win or lose within a four-hour period, organizational leaders must carefully track their goals over the long term. Doing so allows them to ensure that their team members complete daily tasks, while also helping them stay the course of making the work environment more inclusive and welcoming to all employees.

As team members work towards achieving the commendable goal of making the workforce more inclusive, one thing is certain: not all of them will be equally invested in making the goal a reality. Even some people of color will have reservations – they may be resigned to the idea that systemic racism does not just disappear because of good intentions. The team must have some ground rules laid out to ensure that everyone is on the same page – starting with four crucial points of understanding or agreement.

Action + Accountability = Positive Results

At one college where I formerly worked, there were allegations of racial discrimination made against managers in several departments. The college's President – who was new in her role at the time – took quick action to oversee a racial climate assessment which led to our team setting up affinity discussion groups (White, Latinx, Black, and Asian) on the campus. Each affinity group was asked to discuss their feelings and insights about racial injustices that had taken place during the previous ten years. After weeks of holding focus group meetings, and combing through evidence of complaints by faculty, students, and other academic leaders, we held a Town Hall meeting to discuss the investigation's outcomes, inviting all of the college's 2000+ employees and over 25,000 students to attend. The final report was shared with the crowd, along with the conclusion that the complaints were valid, and that they needed to be addressed and resolved. At that moment, a collective exhale could be felt in the room. There were many present who felt validated, and a few men of color literally cried when the President assured everyone that she would do everything in her power to eliminate the negative racial climate. While some members of the staff disagreed with the findings, the meeting was cathartic and deescalated tensions that had been brewing across the campus.

Fast forward to five years later and the college is no long experiencing any racial harassment complaints, and most of the employees are thankful for the actions the college President took to make the campus more inclusive. It took an unwavering commitment on her part, and the involvement of many team members, to make that transformation a reality.

Kindness and Empathy

No matter what happens on the journey to ensuring a better, more inclusive workplace, all employees must realize that everyone should be treated with dignity and respect. It is absolutely vital that everyone fully agrees to protect all others regardless of their color, last name, height, marital status, sexual orientation, and whatever else makes people different. If any individuals do not adhere to this rule, the whole notion of transforming the environment into an inclusive workplace will become little more than a wavering mirage or figment of the imagination.

Research has shown that when people feel psychologically safe, they feel less fear and are more likely to be more productive contributors in the workplace. This has been proven by Dr. Amy Edmondson, Novartis professor of management at the Harvard School of Business who defined a psychologically safe workplace as "one where people are not full of fear, and not trying to cover their tracks to avoid being embarrassed or punished."[21] She further claims, "Without psychological safety, there's a greater risk of cutting corners and people getting hurt, whether employees, customers, or patients." In a work environment where implicit biases have not been confronted or eliminated, people of color will continue to experience racial trauma and abuse. To mitigate the effects of microaggressions, there needs to be a way to hold people accountable for stepping outside the bounds of kindness and treating others unequally in words or deeds.

To get everyone in the same place, there must be a shared agreement on guidelines for what a kind and empathic work environment represents – including examples of what represents unkind words, gestures, or behaviors towards others in the workplace. A great way to formalize what is acceptable and what is not is to draft a "We Exemplify Kindness" document – with the input of all employees – consisting of shared beliefs on how kindness should be modeled in the department. The document should break it down according to the following components of Who (the people in the workplace), what (kindness vs. unkindness), When (workday and every day), Where (workplace and business trips), and How (in our word and actions, while online, offline, or face to face). The Manager should be the initiator, drafting the document along with his or her direct reports, and it should then be shared at a meeting to get everyone's input. There should also be a chance for people who have experienced unkindness or microaggressions to meet privately with the leadership team to outline what issues they have faced in the past. In so doing, the leadership team will find ways to handle future issues that may stem from past aggressions.

Four Power Moves to Achieve the Inclusion Journey with Your Team

Once the 'We are Kindness' document is discussed, revised, approved, and implemented, there can also be strategies planned for responding in the event that someone continues with unkind behaviors toward people of color. The following power moves can be used as proactive measures to achieve positive results:

Power Move #1

Racialized behavior patterns will not instantly disappear once a new DEI initiative is implemented. A wise inclusive leader will find direct reports to serve as allies to people of color in the workplace. These individuals could be given the title of 'Inclusion Ally' or 'D&I Advocate' and assigned the role of stepping up to advocate for people of color when they come under attack in meetings or otherwise. If the Inclusion Ally sees or hears anything unkind, their goal would be to speak to the offender and then bring the incident to the manager's – and possibly HR's – attention. The purpose of this direct intervention is to show the victim that unkind behavior will not be tolerated.

It also indicates that disciplinary action may be taken against the aggressor in the form of a write-up or verbal warning.

The number of advocates necessary will depend on how large the department is: With thirty or fewer workers, one advocate should be sufficient. In a department of sixty to seventy workers, two advocates will suffice, and for ninety to hundred workers, three to four advocates should be appointed. These individuals should be trained and given guidance on how to intervene and settle issues that involve individuals using microaggressions, unkind behavior, or put-downs.

Power Move #2

Instead of putting all of the pressure on the D&I advocates, everyone, even minorities, should be encouraged to take a stand and make their voices heard against any bigotry or racist behavior they witness within the workplace. It is important to educate all team members to help them understand they have a responsibility to speak up if they witness racialized oppression in the workplace. The message they must hear is that if they do not speak up, they are indirectly supporting the negative behavior – and in so doing, they are actually complicit to systemic racism.

Power Move #3

When a person becomes an aggressor against another victim in the department, it should not be swept under the rug and forgotten about. There should always be some form of restoration made between the aggressor and the victim in order to find ways to rebuild trust and make things right between the two. The only way that victims in an organization will feel they can move forward with trust and confidence is if there is follow-through to ensure the action is not committed again without consequences.

Power Move #4

If an aggressor commits such an offence again, they must be dealt with swiftly through progressive discipline in the form of a write-up. Management should also ensure the negative behavior is documented in the person's yearly performance evaluation. If the individual is newly on-boarded and commits a racial offence within their probationary period, they should be put on a one- or two-day administrative leave, with termination occurring if they repeat the offence again before the end of the year.

Beyond Hope and Trust – Checks and Balances

As much as we want to believe that everyone on our team and in our department will be on board and committed to the strategies of creating an inclusive environment, in all honesty, there will be those who will smile, pretend to be on board, but in reality, have no interest in contributing to the endeavor. This behavior is difficult to track and even harder to prove. But to ensure people feel safe if and when negative behaviors surface, you need to establish checks and balances so that people can report anonymously and dodge retribution from those committing the offences.

When employees witness unkindness, mean-spirited words, or other actions that come across as contradictory to the mission of the organization, employees – particularly those who want to be allies to the victims of these assaults – should have a way to anonymously report the incidents to management and HR. The idea behind an anonymous hotline is to hold people accountable for committing micro and macro assaults against others. Providing anonymity is crucial for adding a layer of safety in this process – almost like a home security system, which goes off when someone tries to break in and steal something. A multilayered system like this allows everyone to serve sentry, much like a community watch group monitoring their neighborhood to ensure that no one breaks into someone's home while they are away.

With a system of checks and balances like this, everybody agrees to be a good steward in creating and maintaining a sense of harmony amongst the entire team. Being a good steward means understanding the mission and principles of goodwill that are the organization's brand and being committed to exhibiting behaviors that faithfully reflect good organizational citizenship.

It also calls for everyone to commit to infusing the work environment with the qualities of unity, harmony, and cooperation. This collective commitment requires that everyone remain conscious and mindful of any actions counterproductive to building an organization focused on helping everyone reach their full potential – both as employees and ultimately, as agents of change.

Rewards and Incentives

People are always more motivated to achieve goals when they are rewarded for doing so. Your employees are no different – they like to be recognized and given some form of compensation for standing out for attaining a goal that others could not reach. To keep people motivated to achieve your organization's DEI goals, I suggest clearly mapping out benchmarks of achievement, as well as rewards for those who end up hitting the identified targets.

One way to do this is to ask your employees what they would like to receive (besides money) once they carry out the DEI goals. Rewards could take the form of restaurant or shopping gift cards, or even gift cards they could redeem with local tours operators or entertainment venues. It does not matter so much what the specific rewards are as long as the benchmarks are agreed upon and the rewards are distributed once the goals are achieved. To begin, give certificates to the first five or ten people who complete three strategies. Then, give out higher-level awards to those who complete the entire process. You can also generate other awards along the way, depending on how your process is set out for achieving your DEI goals. You could set aside rewards and incentives, for example, for those who sign up to be Equity Advocates or DEI Allies. You could also reward individuals who organize volunteer events with other organizations in the community, who set up educational events highlighting aspects of Diversity and Inclusion, who arrange excursions to explore other cultures after hours, or even reward those who invite DEI lecturers to visit the department and speak to all the team members.

You could also create an 'over-the-top' award for the one person who ends up modeling and exemplifying what inclusiveness represents at its highest level in the organization. You can involve all your employees in voting for the person who has done the most work and who stands out as having made a major contribution to achieving your organization's DEI goals.

How Do You Know When the Work Environment is Inclusive?

There are several ways to determine whether your work towards achieving DEI goals has positively affected and transformed your work environment. You will want to hone in on how the changes have impacted your minority employees over the course of the past year – their outlook and reflections will tell you a lot. You should also conduct an anonymous qualitative analysis – including written comments – to submit to HR, and then involve a researcher to analyze and report on it.

This is also a great time to break your employees into affinity groups and have them report on changes, challenges, and next steps they feel are imperative for reaching the DEI goals agreed upon the year before. Once the affinity groups meet and share their feelings and insights, have their feedback summarized, and then bring it to a departmental meeting and share it with the larger group. A representative from HR, along with an external DEI consultant, should be on hand to speak with the group, answer questions, and discuss what needs to happen going forward.

Along with the DEI consultant and HR rep, look for themes within each affinity group report to see how the entire process is moving and to determine what stands in the way of any future progress. Once all the reports have been merged, a crucial step is to take that data – including key performance indicators, challenges, and other relevant data –and draft a SWOT analysis. Identifying the Strengths, Weaknesses, Opportunities, and Threats will form a jumping off point for setting and reaching the goals of the upcoming year.

Lastly, the manager and direct reports should convene and determine what positive changes have occurred in the department and what the next steps are to achieve any unmet DEI goals. They will want to look at the goals in the ADAPT plan and ask whether they have all been completed successfully. Have all members gone through the five strategies, and of the ones who have, have they all become allies? Have they developed a collaboration with someone in the department or outside the department? Have they participated in collaboration with a community organization? Even more importantly, have they done anything to confront and tackle a vestige of systemic racism either in or outside the organization? Once these numbers have been quantified and a qualitative report has been completed, the manager will be well positioned to determine what else needs to be done to complete the DEI plan.

CHAPTER 10
COMPLETING YOUR DEI JOURNEY AND MAKING DEI-BASED WORK FUN, CREATIVE, AND ALIVE

Running the DEI marathon will be a long and challenging path, and no one can predict when and how you will achieve all your DEI goals. However, one thing is certain: if the mission is pushed along too rigidly – with no room for fun or creativity – the journey will feel arduous and be much harder to complete. The great thing about organically becoming an inclusive leader is that you have full control over the process of discovering your strengths and weaknesses and figuring out what you need to do to bring yourself up to speed. Just as you will need to go easy on your long-term development in becoming an inclusive leader, you will need to also grant your team members that same leeway.

Staying Engaged with Your DEI Team

As you grow together with your team, you will need to brainstorm about how to keep everyone engaged in achieving your DEI goals, as well as how to keep people motivated beyond the workplace. How do you tap into employees' motivational banks and keep them thinking about how to improve and make the workplace inclusive for everyone? How can you keep this top-of-mind for everyone and ensure it does not dissipate after the first year? In order to succeed, people should be allowed to let their imaginations run wild with creative vigor.

Keeping your team engaged with DEI is about more than just the workplace. It stretches into everyone carrying their cultural competency outside the workplace and practicing it just as authentically outside the organization as they do within it. The work you are doing with your teams will mean they can stop merely listening to what the gurus are saying about D&I and go beyond what is offered to them by the organization. As you engage and motivate your team members, they will be able to independently choose books that interest them or even invite in guests who inspire them to go beyond the confines of the KPIs you chose collectively a year ago.

In a broad sense, people can decide who they want to collaborate and learn with. They can move freely towards creating their own rules of engagement. Beyond working with internal partners, employees can reach out and collaborate with community partners to achieve the same types of goals being pursued within the organization. Employees can work in groups to collaborate with community partners and engage with them in solving community-based issues and vice versa. There are no limits to what can happen to expand inclusivity beyond the department, outside the organization, and past the confines of 9 to 5, Monday through Friday. There are no boundaries for how it can be accomplished, and no limitations on where these interactions can take place. People can let their imaginations run free. More exposure to people and places outside of the organization can lead to new pathways of knowledge that will expand people's connections to people and cultures from all around the world. The one key thing that should not be absent from this journey is the fun and adventure of learning from others, and the objective of working with people to accomplish mutually beneficial goals.

Models of Workplace Inclusion – How Should It Look?

People typically interact mostly with others who look like them. Before the ADAPT method is implemented, workers primarily interact among their affinity groups both within and outside of the workplace. Beyond that, you do not see them stepping outside of racialized safe zones or doing things with others from outside of the organization. One of the distinguishing features of inclusiveness becoming a reality, though, is that people can operate comfortably outside their affinity groups. If, after one year, you see employees taking extra steps to invite people from outside their affinity groups to join them for meals or to attend after-hours social events, you can view it as a social transformation in the workplace. In addition to this being a major turning point, an even bigger transformation is when people break out of their racialized safety and comfort zones and invite others into their churches, entertainment venues, and homes.

A study conducted by the Public Religion Research Institute in 2014 showed that 91 percent of the average White American's closest friends and family members are White, and just 1 percent are Black. While Black Americans tended to have a more diverse social network, the number of White friends was far less than expected. The average African American has 83 percent Black confidants, 8 percent White confidants, 2 percent Latino confidants, zero Asian confidants, and 3 percent mixed-race confidants. One of the most glaring statistics from the study showed that when asked to name their closest friends and family members, 75 percent of White Americans did not name even one person who was not White.[22]

Similar results were evident when Canadians were asked about the state of race relations in their country. While a good portion of White Canadians believe that race relations are improving in their country, the percentage of people holding that opinion declines among racialized groups, especially amongst Chinese, South Asians and Black Canadians. The study concluded that since George Floyd's death, racial minorities in Canada have become hyper-sensitive to the discrimination they face in Canada

– and that they are frustrated about the slow pace of change towards creating equal opportunities for all in their country.

These two studies reveal that North American minorities still feel excluded, and it is a reality that the discrimination they face carries over into the workplace. What does this mean for the aspiring inclusive leader? They must be aware that racial minorities carry a heavy burden of 'integration-fatigue' during organizational onboarding, the weight of which will not dissipate unless their work environment is inclusive and welcoming. This can only take place if team members evolve and confront their implicit biases.

Mentoring and Delegation Opportunities

Another obvious sign of success with building inclusivity will be the broader interaction of diverse team members. Look for increased levels of mentoring where more managers and leaders are supporting minorities with growing and succeeding in the workplace. Most White managers faithfully and committedly mentor their own, but in a fully inclusive work environment, mentorship opportunities should be equal. There should also be fewer equity gaps than before the inclusivity campaign began.

Other bits of evidence to look for are fewer microaggressions being committed against visible minorities – the absence of which should lead to a higher sense of belonging in the department, fewer tensions, and more unity.

Successful efforts at building inclusion should have resulted in fewer complaints being filed with HR, leading to less overall attrition and fewer minority staff members leaving the organization out of discontent or an inability to deal with maltreatment. The final proof of inclusivity success should be that minorities excel in their jobs and are being fairly promoted to higher-level jobs alongside their White peers. This will be undeniable proof that the effects of equity and inclusivity are at work and that they are profoundly influencing the department's overall productivity.

Final Thoughts on Being the Quintessential Inclusive Manager

Many great books have been written over the years about going from good to great as a manager or organizational leader. Some of the groundbreaking bestsellers sold to aspiring managers include *The One Minute Manager, The 7 Habits of Highly Effective People, Good to Great*, and many more. Although these books describe the unique skills needed to lead and manage organizations, they share little information about how to become an inclusive leader, primarily because there was not a huge focus on leading diverse employee populations in the 1960s through the early 2000s when these books were published. Back then, the prevailing attitude was that minorities should assimilate when they were on boarded into corporations. They were expected to take on the ideal employee's primary physical and mental characteristics.

When I interned for IBM back in the 1980s, the dream of every student who majored in business was to walk through those squeaky-clean doors wearing the quintessential blue power suit and crisply ironed white shirt and be accepted by the top brass. In those days, the more closely you resembled the IBM replica, the better; that expectation applied equally to both women and men. For African Americans, long natural hairstyles were frowned upon, just as wearing dreads or cornrows would have led to immediate dismissal. Black women who wanted to rise through the ranks of companies like IBM had to wear their hair straight and men were pressured to wear their hair short if they wanted to be promoted to higher-level jobs.

Things have changed drastically since then. With the rise of the BLM movement and the death of George Floyd, public opinion about racial equality has grown exponentially, and pressures to honor the cultural and ethnic differences of others – while getting the job done – is the new zeitgeist of this era. As we move into a new age of Diversity and Inclusion, there are many key qualities and behaviors for inclusive managers to model:

Unity: Inclusive leaders will put a high premium on keeping the group unified, and they will strive to ensure that estrangement and apathy are not allowed to pervade the workplace.

Transparency: Ensuring there are no hidden agendas and people are kept in the loop. Information should be shared often, and no one should be prevented from being informed of opportunities for advancement.

Professional development: Making sure that people are informed on best practices in the area of equity and inclusion and that all elements of training are high-level, engaging, and super informative.

Recognition: Employees are recognized and rewarded for their progress in attaining DEI goals that are set for the department.

Microaggressions are confronted and taken down immediately: Everyone will apply an all-hands-on-deck attitude when it comes to ridding the workplace of insults, racial vitriol, and mini-condemnations against people of color in the workplace.

Violations will be called out: Making sure that when aggressions are committed, they are nipped in the bud and not repeated.

Mentoring and advancing the careers of people of color: Ensuring that all employees are mentored equitably and that advancement opportunities are shared with all.

Modeling collaborations with other cultural groups internally and externally: Showing and demonstrating what cultural collaboration looks like.

Striking down all forms of systemic racism in the workplace – including words, actions, and symbols.

Being an ally and defending minorities against discriminatory practices and behavior.

Making DEI Activities Fun

These qualities and behaviors can and should be practiced interchangeably by aspiring inclusive managers. Doing one without the others will not successfully transform the workplace into a safe and trusted environment for people of color – it is critical that the inclusive leader demonstrate a full and absolute commitment to the transformation. Their success will not happen in isolation though – without the engagement and participation of the majority of the team, the operation will stall, and the team will be incapable of leveraging its full potential. Only when the manager gets everyone to play their part and understand the mission and vision, will things move forward. Every team member must understand why their input is meaningful for developing success with building inclusivity at all levels of the organization.

Seeing the End in the Beginning

Strong organizational leaders often have a penchant for thinking that they alone can lead their team to the proverbial Promised Land. They also think that the loftier the goals, the more essential it is for people to look to them for guidance on navigating the waters and reaching the finish line. However, the path to diversity, equity, and inclusion is one that most managers and executive leaders have neither read nor learned much about. Many will have studied at length about leading within an organizational framework, but determining how to change their behaviors to become more inclusive is a new phenomenon – one that requires deeper, more personal reflection.

Unpacking what an inclusive workplace should look and feel like – and determining how to motivate its employees to strive for excellence – will require more than a singular vision. It will require many unique visions – drawn from many different perspectives –combined into one harmonious vision and articulating a singular message for all to hear. That vision will proclaim loudly what everyone in the department desires in an inclusive work environment – what it will offer them, as well as the others who will one day occupy that space. This vision will speak for all of the voices and mindsets in the room – past, present, and future. It will honor the people from the past who were not allowed to work in a space that honored the human values of kindness, trust, and belonging. It will also provide the foundation for current employees who aspire to build a place where future employees will be happy to benefit in ways their predecessors could not.

This multi-faceted vision will not come from an HR textbook or be based on the external ideas of those who are not present in the workspace. It will reflect the desires of those who exist in the present moment and in the current workplace. It will become a blueprint for guiding everyone's behavior towards bringing about unity, trust, and organizational prosperity.

Negative behaviors that lead to disunity should be visualized and excluded from the safe space being envisioned. Just as Native Americans regard their living spaces as sacred, holy ground to be openly utilized to raise the spiritual consciousness of everyone associated with the tribe, the workplace should be viewed as a space for people to exponentialize their fullest potential. It should not be filled with toxicity, negativity, or cultural conflict. Instead, it should motivate people to come to work so that they can excel in ways that will serve humanity.

The Vision of Unity-N-Diversity in the Workplace

The workplace should be exhilarating to the extent that it strongly supports everyone with achieving his or her fullest potential. With an unwavering commitment to setting the vision and doing the work, unity and diversity will be achieved. This is not a vision to splash haphazardly on a proverbial canvas – it must be painted with striking courage, loving care, diligent forbearance, bright awareness, and unwavering ambition. When people behold this multi-colored vision, they will see it is not monopolized by any one viewpoint, whether Black, White, LatinX, LGBTQ, female, male, neuro-divergent, learning disabled, or physically handicapped. Instead, it will encompass the images of all those who participated in offering their understanding of inclusivity from the deep perspective of human empathy. This empathy connects the hearts and minds of people who have suffered, but who love deeply from the depths of their souls.

This image can serve as a blueprint – one that is world embracing and encompassing all the feelings and aspirations of those people serving in the workplace. If carried out honestly and humbly, the visions emanating from each person involved will blend the obscure wishes of the few with the dominant wishes of the many. This unique vision will protect, defend, and be the voice of the voiceless. It will also be the ongoing conscience of the righteous who believe all should be granted equal rights and dignity based on the constitutional framework of the institution's mission to uphold racial justice. Bringing this vision to fruition is a significant undertaking, much the same way that giving birth to a new child is a major undertaking – one that is carefully orchestrated by a doctor, nurses, and medical technicians. Everyone working on this vision is important, and no one's contributions can be overlooked or dismissed; the blueprint of this unique and emerging work environment will only be as strong as each person's willingness to offer the best of themselves to achieve equity for all.

ABOUT THE AUTHOR

Dr. Jonathan King brings over three decades of expertise in providing customized Diversity, Equity, and Inclusion (DEI) Training to Executive leaders and Middle managers in companies, non-profit organizations, and institutions of higher learning. Dr. King is very passionate and committed to the idea of building unity among all constituencies and stakeholders within the organization, and he has successfully trained employees throughout the U.S. and around the globe, including, Japan, Canada, and Africa. Dr. King has served in different leadership roles within Fortune 500 Companies (i.e. Sony Entertainment, Warner International), various NGO's, and Institutions of Higher Learning. He holds a bachelor's degree in Business, a master's degree in Educational Administration from Harvard University, a master's degree in International Relations from the International University of Japan, and a Ph.D. in Educational Leadership. Dr. King is the CEO and President of JTK International Consulting LLC, a strategic development solutions firm that specializes in organizational transformation, diversity, equity, and inclusion, implicit bias, leadership excellence, and personal and professional development.

Contact Jonathan to speak at your event at:

www.JKingConsulting.com

[1] https://www.mckinsey.com/~/media/mckinsey/featured%20insights/diversity%20and%20inclusion/diversity%20wins%20how%20inclusion%20matters/ diversity-wins-how-inclusion-matters-vf.pdf

[2]   https://www.mckinsey.com/~/media/mckinsey/featured%20insights/diversity%20and%20inclusion/diversity%20wins%20how%20inclusion%20 20matters/diversity-wins-how-inclusion-matters-vf.pdf

[3]   https://www.bcg.com/en-ca/publications/2018/how-diverse-leadership-teams-boost-innovation

[4]   https://www.greatplacetowork.com/resources/blog/workplace-diversity-might-be-the-key-to-surviving-recession

[5] https://leaders.com/articles/social-issues/inclusive-leadership/
[6]   https://www2.deloitte.com/us/en/insights/topics/talent/six-signature-traits-of-inclusive-leadership.html

[7] Greenwald & Banaji, 1995

[8] Pierce, 1970

[9]   https://williamsinstitute.law.ucla.edu/publications/lgbt-workplacediscrimination/

[10]   https://www.mckinsey.com/capabilities/people-and-organizational-performance/our-insights/lgbtq-plus-voices-learning-from-lived-experiences
[11]   https://www.yahoo.com/news/several-torrance-police-officerslinked-130044640.html

[12] https://implicit.harvard.edu/implicit/

[13]   https://www.businessinsider.com/every-company-that-was-sued-discrimination-and-harassment-lawsuits-2020-2021-1

[14] 14   https://www.cnn.com/2019/09/30/success/dallas-mavericks-ceo-cynthia-marshall-boss-files/index.html

[15] https://stories.starbucks.com/stories/inclusion-diversity/

[16] https://bebs.org/7-companies-promoting-diversity-and-inclusion-in-the-workplace/

[17] https://www.vox.com/2018/4/18/17242788/chastity-jones-dreadlock-job-discrimination

[18] https://www.latimes.com/local/lanow/la-pol-ca-natural-hair-discrimination-bill-20190703-story.html

[19] Gundling & Williams, p. 154

[20] https://bigthink.com/plus/inclusion-in-the-workplace/

[21] https://www.forbes.com/sites/shanesnow/2020/05/04/how-psychological-safety-actually-works

[22] https://www.prri.org/research/poll-race-religion-politics-americans-social-networks/